Praise for Tim Ma[...]
The Age of Walls

"Marshall is a skilled explainer of the world as it is, and geography buffs will be pleased by his latest."
—*Kirkus Reviews*

"A timely and exhilarating clamber over the walls of history."
—Peter Frankopan, author of *The Silk Roads*

"A readable primer to many of the biggest problems facing the world."
—*Daily Express* (UK)

"Accomplished, well-researched, and pacey . . . For anyone who wants to look beyond the headlines and explore the context of some of the biggest challenges facing the world today, it is a fascinating and fast read."
—*City A.M.* (UK)

"[Marshall] writes with the cool drollery that characterized the work of Christopher Hitchens or Simon Winchester."
—*USA Today*

"Fans of geography, history, and politics (and maps) will be enthralled."
—*Fort Worth Star-Telegram*

"Marshall's insistence on seeing the world through the lens of geography compels a fresh way of looking at maps—not just as objects for orientation or works of art, but as guideposts to the often thorny relations between nations."
—*The New York Times Book Review*

"Marshall is excellent on some of the highways and byways of geopolitics."
—*Financial Times*

"An incisive, meticulous survey of humanity's physical barriers . . . This enlightening shred assessment of the walls that separate us proves that there is actually far more that unites us."
—*Booklist* (starred review)

THE AGE OF WALLS

How Barriers Between Nations
Are Changing Our World

TIM MARSHALL

SCRIBNER

New York   London   Toronto   Sydney   New Delhi

Scribner
An Imprint of Simon & Schuster, Inc.
1230 Avenue of the Americas
New York, NY 10020

Picture credits: Pages 10–11: iStock.com/real444; pages 38–39: Herika Martinez/AFP/
Getty Images; pages 70–71: iStock.com/Joel Carillet; pages 98–99: Ahmad Al-Rubaye/
Stringer/Getty Images; pages 122–23: STRDEL/AFP/Getty Images; pages 154–55:
Stefano Montesi/Corbis News/Getty Images; pages 182–83: *Washington Post*/Getty
Images; pages 218–19: Epics/Hulton Archive/Getty Images.

Sources for maps: Page 19 and 24: *Economist*/2010 China census; page 47: Open-
streetmap.org; page 59: Pew Research Center; page 106 and 107: CRS, Pew Research
Center, *CIA World Factbook*; page 136: *Diercke International Atlas*; page 165:
John Bartholomew & Co.; page 235: BBC.

Maps: JP Map Graphics Ltd.

Dedicated to my mother, Margaret McDonald,
and a life spent building bridges

Contents

Introduction

The border wall between Israel and the West Bank is among the most forbidding and hostile in the world. Viewed from up close, whichever side you find yourself on, it rears up from the ground, overwhelming and dominating you. Faced by this blank expanse of steel and concrete, you are dwarfed not only by its size but by what it represents. You are on one side; "they" are on the other.

Thirty years ago a wall came down, ushering in what looked like a new era of openness and internationalism. In 1987 President Ronald Reagan went to the Brandenburg Gate in divided Berlin and called out to his opposite number in the Soviet Union, "Mr. Gorbachev—tear down this wall!" Two years later it fell. Berlin, Germany, and then Europe were united once more. In those heady times, some intellectuals predicted an end of history. However, history does not end.

In recent years, the cry "Tear down this wall" is losing the argument against "fortress mentality." It is struggling to be heard, unable to compete with the frightening heights of mass migration, the backlash against globalization, the resurgence of nationalism, the collapse of communism, and the 9/11 attacks and their aftermath. These are the fault lines that will shape our world for years to come.

We are seeing walls being built along borders everywhere. Despite globalization and advances in technology, we seem to be feeling more divided than ever. Thousands of miles of walls and fences have gone up around the world in the twenty-first century. At least sixty-five countries, more than a third of the world's nation-states, have built barriers along their borders; half of those erected since World War II sprang up between 2000 and now. Within a few years the European nations could have more miles of walls, fences, and barriers on their borders than there were at the height of the Cold War. They began by separating Greece and Macedonia, Macedonia and Serbia, and Serbia and Hungary, and as we became less shocked by each stretch of barbed wire, others followed suit—Slovenia began building on the Croatian border, the Austrians fenced off Slovenia, and Sweden put up barriers to prevent illegal immigrants crossing from Denmark, while Estonia, Latvia, and Lithuania have all started on defensive fortifications on their borders with Russia.

Europe is certainly not alone. The UAE has built a fence along its border with Oman, Kuwait likewise with Iraq. Iraq and Iran maintain a physical divide, as do Iran and Pakistan—all 435 miles of it. In Central Asia, Uzbekistan, despite being landlocked, has closed itself off from its five neighbors: Afghanistan, Tajikistan, Kazakhstan, Turkmenistan, and Kyrgyzstan. The border with Tajikistan is even mined. And on the story goes, through the barriers separating Brunei and Malaysia, Malaysia and Thailand, Pakistan and India, India and Bangladesh, China and North Korea, North and South Korea, and so on around the world.

We erect walls for many reasons because we are divided in many ways—in wealth, race, religion, and politics. Sometimes divisions lead to violence, and walls are erected to protect or defend. Sometimes walls go up to keep certain people out. Sometimes physical walls don't go up at all, but we still feel the separation; it's in our minds. These invisible barriers are often just as effective.

These walls tell us much about international politics, but the anxieties they represent transcend the nation-state boundaries on which they sit. The primary purpose of the walls appearing throughout Europe is to stop the wave of migrants—but they also say much about wider divisions and instability in the structure of the European Union and within its member nations. President Trump's proposed wall along the US-Mexico border is intended to stem the flow of migrants from the south, but it also taps into a wider fear many of its supporters feel about changing demographics.

Division shapes politics at every level—the personal, local, national, and international. It's essential to be aware of what has divided us, and what continues to do so, in order to understand what's going on in the world today.

Picture the beginning of Stanley Kubrick's 1968 sci-fi masterpiece, *2001: A Space Odyssey*, the sequence titled "The Dawn of Man." On the African savanna in the prehistoric era, a small tribe of proto-man/apes are drinking peacefully at a watering hole when another tribe turns up. The individuals are quite happy to share with their own group—but not with this new, "other" tribe. A shrieking match ensues in which the new group succeeds in taking over the watering hole, forcing the others to retreat. At this point, if the newcomers had had the nous to make a few bricks and mix some cement, they could have walled off their new possession and guarded it. But given that this is set a few million years ago, they have to fight it out again when the first tribe returns some days later, having boned up on warfare, to reclaim its territory.

Grouping into tribes, feeling alarmed by a lot of outsiders, or responding to perceived threats are very human things to do. We form ties that are important for survival, but also for social cohesion. We develop a group identity, and this often leads to conflict with others. Our groups are competing for resources, but with an element of identity conflict also—a narrative of "us and them."

In the early history of mankind, we were hunter-gatherers: we had not settled or acquired permanent fixed resources that others might covet. Then, in parts of what we now call Turkey and the

Middle East, humans started farming. Instead of roaming far and wide to find food or graze livestock, they plowed the fields and waited for the results. Suddenly (in the context of evolution) more and more of us needed to build barriers: walls and roofs to house ourselves and our livestock, fences to mark our territory, fortresses to retreat to if the territory was overrun, and guards to protect the new system. The Age of Walls was upon us and has long gripped our imagination ever since. We still tell each other tales of the walls of Troy, Jericho, Babylon, Great Zimbabwe, Constantinople, and of the Great Wall of China, Hadrian's Wall, the Inca Walls in Peru, and many others. On and on they stretch, through time, region, and culture, to the present—but now they are electrified, topped with searchlights and CCTV.

These physical divisions are mirrored by those in the mind— the great ideas that have guided our civilizations and given us identity and a sense of belonging—such as the Great Schism of Christianity, the split of Islam into Sunni and Shia, and in more recent history the titanic battles between communism, fascism, and democracy.

The title of Thomas Friedman's 2005 book, *The World Is Flat*, was based on the belief that globalization would inevitably bring us closer together. It has done that, but it has also inspired us to build barriers. When faced with perceived threats—the financial crisis, terrorism, violent conflict, refugees and immigration, the increasing gap between rich and poor—people cling more tightly to their groups. The cofounder of Facebook, Mark Zuckerberg, believed social media would unite us. In some respects it has, but it has simultaneously given voice and organizational ability to new cyber tribes, some of whom spend their time spewing invective and division across the World Wide Web. There seem now to be as many tribes, and as much conflict between them, as there have ever been. The question we face today is, What form do our modern tribes take? Do we define ourselves by class, by race, by religion, by nationality? And is it possible for these tribes to coexist in a world where the concept of "us and them" remains?

It all comes down to this "us and them" concept and the walls we build in our minds. Sometimes the "other" has a different language or skin color; a different religion or other set of beliefs. One example of this came up recently when I was in London with a group of thirty leading young journalists from around the world whom I was helping to train. I'd mentioned the Iran-Iraq War, in which up to 1 million Iranians had died, and had used the possibly clumsy phrase "Muslims killing Muslims." A young Egyptian journalist jumped from his chair and shouted that he could not allow me to say this. I pointed out the statistics from that terrible war and he replied, "Yes, but the Iranians are not Muslims."

The penny dropped, along with my heart. The majority of Iranians are Shia, so I asked him, "Are you saying that the Shia are not Muslims?"

"Yes. The Shia are not Muslims."

Such divisions do not come down to competition for resources, but rather to a claim that what you think is the only truth, and those with differing views are lesser people. With such certainty of superiority, the walls quickly go up. If you introduce competition for resources, they go up higher. We seem to be in that place now.

For the purpose of this book I use walls as shorthand for barriers, fences, and divisions in all their variety. We do look at physical walls in each chapter, most of which involve bricks and mortar, or concrete and wire, but those walls are the "what" of division, not the why—and they are just the beginning of the story.

I haven't been able to cover every divided region. Instead I have focused on those that best illustrate the challenges of identity in a globalized world: the effects of migration (the USA, Europe, the Indian subcontinent); nationalism as a force for both unity and division (China, the UK, Africa); and the intersections of religion and politics (Israel, the Middle East).

In China, we see a strong nation-state with a number of divisions within its borders—such as regional unrest and wealth disparity—that pose a risk to national unity, threatening economic progress and power; thus the government must exert control over the Chinese people. The USA is also divided, for different reasons: the era of Trump has exacerbated race relations in the Land of the Free, but has also revealed a hitherto unrivaled split between Republicans and Democrats, who are more opposed than ever before.

It sometimes seems as if it's easier to divide than unite. For example, the myriad complexities of how to put Korea back together were brought into focus by the sketchy agreement between the North and South on denuclearization in the spring of 2018. There were vague murmurings of eventual reunification included in the "Panmunjom Declaration for Peace, Prosperity and Unification of the Korean Peninsula." These were in the spirit of the declaration, but the realities of geopolitics soon kicked in. There are five players in this game and each has a different view of the future.

The USA's imperative is to prevent North Korea from being able to reach it with a nuclear weapon. However, maintaining a military presence in South Korea is also important to counter China's growing naval power in the Yellow Sea and elsewhere. This latter point does not fit with Chinese strategy, nor with North Korea's ideas about dominating the peninsula, and this of course runs counter to South Korea's interests. Meanwhile the Japanese, who host their own US military bases, would be alarmed at the prospect of a unified Korea, especially one under Chinese influence, as it views the peninsula as a buffer between it and China.

These complexities serve as a reminder when we look at the partitions, walls, and divides in this book as to why it is so hard to overcome them at the political level.

The divisions between Israel and Palestine are well established, but with so many further subdivisions within each population it is almost impossible to try to agree upon a solution. Religious and ethnic divisions also spark violence across the Middle East, highlighting the key struggle between Shia and Sunni Muslims—each incident is the result of complex factors, but much of it comes down to religion, especially the regional rivalry between Saudi Arabia and Iran. On the Indian subcontinent, population movements, now and in the coming years, reveal the plight of those fleeing religious persecution as well as that of the many economic and climate refugees.

In Africa, the borders left behind by colonialism are proving difficult to reconcile with tribal identities that remain strong. Across Europe the very concept of the EU is under threat as the walls go back up, proving that the differences of the Cold War years haven't entirely been resolved, and that nationalism has never gone away in the age of internationalism. And as the UK leaves the EU, Brexit reveals divisions throughout the kingdom—long-established regional identities, as well as the more recent social and religious tensions that have formed in the era of globalization.

In a time of fear and instability, people will continue to group together, to protect themselves against perceived threats. Those threats don't just come from the borders. They can also come from within.

CHAPTER 1

China

As in the real world, freedom and order are both necessary in cyberspace.

—President Xi Jinping

Previous pages: The Great Wall of China is more than thirteen thousand miles long, running roughly along the border between central China and Inner Mongolia.

C hinese emperors always struggled to unite their disparate and divided fiefdoms into a unitary whole. President Xi Jinping is no different. He may not be called emperor, but his official titles give the game away—General Secretary of the Communist Party of China, President of the People's Republic of China, Chairman of the Central Commission for Integrated Military and Civilian Development—the list goes on and on. In early 2018 he moved to abolish the rules limiting presidential tenures in office to two terms. He's not just a Supreme Leader, he's a Very Supreme Leader.

Everything about what he leads is vast, including the challenges. China's five geographical time zones amount to an area the size of the USA. Within this space live 1.4 billion ethnically diverse people, speaking dozens of different languages; it's a multiethnic empire with Communist Chinese characteristics. There may be five geographic time zones, but only one is official. The answer to "What's the time?" is "Whatever time Beijing says it is." This central rule has long been the case, but the twenty-first-century emperor has a luxury few of his precursors enjoyed. He can survey his empire from the air—not just the area encompassed by the Himalayas, to the Sea of Japan and the Gobi Desert, down to the South China Sea, but now the economic empire spanning the globe.

Xi is good at quietly projecting his power. He travels more than many of his predecessors. He flies to the world's capitals, confident in the united economic power of the new China, but en route to the airport he will be reminded of how careful Chinese leaders must always be to ensure that the center holds.

As you drive northeast along the Airport Expressway out of Beijing toward the Great Wall of China, the divisions within the population are at first difficult for an outsider to identify, but then become increasingly easy. Xi can see these at a glance because many have arisen in his lifetime, some under his leadership.

From the city center, with its gleaming, neon-lit temples to consumerism and upscale apartment buildings for the well-off, the road leads on past miles of high-rise flats inhabited by the ever-burgeoning middle class. Farther out are the factory and industrial workers who, year on year, continue to flow in from the countryside to the capital and other big cities. A local can spot which apartment blocks house the better off, and which have been hastily thrown up to cope with the influx. Once one is out into the small towns and villages, there is little neon and less commercialization. In this part of China the towns are drab, colorless, spartan affairs with few amenities; to the foreign eye, the overwhelming sense is only of grayness. This is perhaps China's greatest divide—that between the urban and rural, the rich and poor—and as we will later see, it worries the ruling Communist Party. It knows that the unity and stability of the People's Republic depend to a great extent on bridging the gap, and that its iron grip on the people will slip if it fails to do so.

Unity has always been crucial to China's success, and at the same time one of its biggest challenges. In the past, the one thing that played both a physical and symbolic role in unifying the country was the Great Wall of China. If Xi kept going along the expressway, straight past the airport, he'd end up on an eight-lane highway heading farther northeast, and from there arrive at a structure that has gripped the world's imagination.

As you approach the Mutianyu section of the Great Wall, the highway diminishes into a simple two-lane road; the buildings become fewer and the landscape increasingly verdant. A few miles away from the wall, the road leads to a parking lot where you must transfer to a coach to take you to where the road ends. Then it's either a cable car to the top or a steep two-mile hike, possibly accompanied by a herd of goats. The unguided goat tour is not optional—if the goats want to follow you, they will; if they don't, they won't. Whichever route you choose, you will eventually see something that makes the effort more than worthwhile.

When I first gazed over the miles of brickwork snaking along the mountaintops, I was not as overawed as I had been at, say, the Grand Canyon. Nor did I feel overwhelmed, as I was by the world's tallest building, Burj Khalifa, in Dubai. I did not feel political ideology emanating from it, as I did when I visited the Berlin Wall at the height of the Cold War. But there was something else. I felt, rightly or wrongly, that I understood China just a little bit better than before.

It didn't make me any sort of expert—far from it—but in that moment I had a much better appreciation of phrases such as *ancient culture* and *the greatest feat in human history*, and of the concept that many in the People's Republic still divide the world into those who are Chinese and those who are not. After all, the wall was built around a simplistic idea: on one side of it was civilization and on the other barbarity.

Behind me, to the south, lay the heartland of the Middle Kingdom, populated by the Han people. To the north, in the far distance beyond the mountains, was where the steppe and desert of Mongolia began, flanked on the right by Manchuria and on the left by the Xinjiang region.

Before the wall existed, some twenty-five hundred years ago, the northern mountains offered a degree of protection to the Han, who had developed settled societies in the fertile lands of the North China Plain. But raiding parties, and occasionally whole armies, from all three regions would find ways through the mountain passes into the flat agricultural lands of the feudal states and cities such as Beijing, Luoyang, and Kaifeng. So, over centuries, the Chinese would develop the quintessential symbol of "us and them."

The great American sinologist John King Fairbank had perhaps one of the best descriptions of the Great Wall, calling it "a line of demarcation separating the steppe from the sown field, nomadism from agriculture, and barbarism from civilization." This fits with the prevailing attitude of "Sinocentrism" at the time—the belief that China was the cultural center on earth, and the most advanced civilization. The Han also believed that China's emperor was the only ruler on earth who was mandated by heaven itself, and thus the legitimate emperor of the world. It therefore followed that not only were all other rulers subordinate, but that all other civilizations were inferior. Near neighbors of different ethnicities were to be brought under the rule of the emperor, although they could have their own local leaders. Nearby barbarian states could have kings, but they had to recognize that they were lesser than the Chinese emperor. Even places farther afield, such as Xinjiang, Java, and Japan, were deemed "tributary states" and had to pay tribute to the Middle Kingdom. This was not a worldview designed to win friends, but it certainly influenced people, and for long periods it worked.

Over the centuries, the Great Wall enhanced China's security, binding it as a political entity and providing the stability to develop farmland in western and northern regions. As the wall stretched westward, it also protected part of the Silk Road, thus furthering economic growth. At its longest, and including the parallel walls, the defensive system stretched for more than thirteen thousand miles. To give a sense of its magnitude, that is equivalent to four walls parallel to each other, each stretching from the East Coast of the USA all the way across to the Pacific Ocean, with a lot of bricks to spare.

Although the physical role it played in uniting the country diminished over the years, it remained an important symbol in the national consciousness. So much so that after the Communists came to power in 1949, Mao Zedong mentioned the wall in a poem about the Long March titled "Mount Liupan," which includes the line: "If we fail to reach the Great Wall we are not true men." The wording of this line has subsequently been adapted into a popular proverb that says, "One who fails to reach the Great Wall is no hero," meaning "If you can't overcome great difficulties, you're no hero."

The poem caused some problems in the new regime, as the Communists seemed to have conflicting views of the wall—many saw it as a symbol of the nation's feudal past and believed it should be consigned to history, even encouraging people to vandalize it. But, given that Mao had written about it, other Communists wanted to visit it to show "Chairman Mao spirit." If you go to the Mutianyu section, you can see written in gigantic white characters on the mountaintop, "Loyalty to Chairman Mao." And the wall was mentioned in the national anthem, adopted in 1949, so the Party clearly recognized its cultural and historical importance. For the most part, they settled for ignoring it—to begin with, at least. During the Cultural Revolution, however, the most fervent of the Red Guards actively destroyed sections of the wall—to them it was a part of the "Four Olds," which had no place in the new China: Old Customs, Old Culture, Old Habits, and Old Ideas.

Mao died in 1976, and with him the Cultural Revolution. After 1978 the new leader, Deng Xiaoping, began a methodical reconstruction of the wall. He started slowly—the early post-Mao years were a time for caution—but by 1984 he was confident enough to pronounce, "Let us love our China and restore our Great Wall." In this endeavor, Deng likely had one eye on tourism and foreign currency; the Communist leadership was beginning to embrace aspects of capitalism and was well aware of how far China had fallen behind other parts of the world. Laws were passed to make it illegal to damage, remove, or write graffiti on any part of the wall, alongside attempts at rebuilding (with mixed success) and a drive toward attracting visitors.

The Great Wall has played a huge role in the popular imagination of both the Chinese and the rest of the world—although some historians argue that the Europeans were more obsessed by it than the Chinese themselves and that this contributed toward awareness of, and identification with, the structure in China itself. So the wall has been instrumental in defining China from outside as well as within its own confines.

The wall was only ever partially successful militarily. Without doubt its early-warning system, fortifications, and strategic strongholds offered some protection, but these were hardly impregnable. However, its role as a symbol of defense, of dividing the Han from the "outsiders," was invaluable; today it remains an icon of a great and ancient culture.

But what of the great and modern culture?

Qin Shi Huang, the founder of the Qin dynasty, succeeded in uniting seven warring states into one China in 221 BCE, but just because it has lasted twenty-three centuries does not automatically mean it will last another.

The Chinese do not like to talk to outsiders about the country's problems or divisions. Whereas you'll not have to go far to find people in Britain or France, say, who will happily tell you their country is going to the dogs, in China it is considered unpatriotic and a loss of face to criticize the state. It might also be risky given that China remains a one-party dictatorship.

Nevertheless, the twenty-three provinces, four municipalities, five autonomous regions, and two special administrative regions have problems and divisions. One of the biggest is that between the Han heartland and the non-Han areas that surround it in a semicircle. To the northeast is Manchuria, to the north Inner Mongolia, to the northwest Xinjiang, and to the west Tibet. These regions are crucial for security, natural resources, and trade, but they aren't all in favor of Chinese rule. Manchuria is now totally dominated by the Han, but the other regions maintain their own identity, language, customs, and, in the cases of Xinjiang and Tibet, their own religions (Islam and Buddhism) and separatist movements.

China has tried to control Xinjiang and its Uighur people for several centuries, but the population has never fully accepted domination by Beijing. There were a series of uprisings in the eighteenth and nineteenth centuries and even a short-lived Eastern Turkestan Republic in the 1930s. Mao annexed Xinjiang in 1949, and it now accounts for about one-sixth of China's territory. To give an idea of how barren and sparsely populated Xinjiang is, it is about half the size of India but with less than 2 percent of its population.

Distribution of the Han population across China's provinces (2010).

The intervening years have seen a mass movement of Han
settlers into Xinjiang, and in a few years' time they are likely to
compose almost half the population, currently at 22 million. This
has not gone unopposed. The Uighurs complain that they are
excluded from the better jobs and persecuted by militia formed
within state-controlled construction industries, and there are
occasional riots and ethnic clashes. Opposition is sometimes
conducted through the legal system, but also via a small terrorist
campaign, partially fueled by Muslim fighters who have returned
from Iraq and Syria. Jihadist organizations in the Central Asian
republics are thought to assist them with money and, if necessary,
safe havens. Alarm bells began to ring when the IS terror group
released a video showing Uighur men training in Iraq, vowing
to plant their flag in China, and threatening that blood would
"flow in rivers."

In the spring of 2017 ethnic violence broke out in the area
between Uighur and Han. This was followed by a massive show
of force by heavily armed government troops. The regional Communist Party leader recommended that the soldiers "bury the
corpses of terrorists in the vast sea of the people's war." President
Xi was somewhat more restrained, contenting himself with a call
for a "Great Wall of Iron" to be built to safeguard Xinjiang and
a warning that ethnic division would not be tolerated—"Just as
one loves one's own eyes, one must love ethnic unity," he said.

Despite the unrest, there is little chance of Beijing's loosening
its iron grip. The region is a buffer zone, is on the new Silk Road
and so is crucial for trade, and has large reserves of the coal that
energy-hungry China so badly needs. But even so, the authorities
are seriously concerned about events there. Such divisions and
dissension undermine the Communist Party's image as the only
source of power and protector of the people.

The same goes for Tibet. Strategically it serves as a buffer
zone for the heartland, preventing India from dominating the

high ground along its border with China—arguably, the Himalayas act as a barrier, which is perhaps why a major conflict has
never emerged between the two nations. This also allows China
to protect its water sources—Tibet is sometimes called the Asian
Water Tower as so many major rivers flow out of the region.

If you measure Tibet by the three Tibetan provinces, it is about
965,000 square miles, or nearly four times the size of France, and
thus equals about a quarter of China's landmass. However, when
Beijing refers to Tibet, it means the Tibet Autonomous Region,
which was established after China defeated the Tibetan army
in 1950. It is less than half the size of the original three provinces, as the rest of the area became absorbed by other Chinese
regions, and it contains only a third of China's ethnically Tibetan
population.

As with the Uighur Muslims, the Tibetan Buddhists retain
a strong sense of identity separate from the Han Chinese. But
for both regions, any hope of self-rule has almost disappeared.
In Tibet, it's estimated that half the population are now Han.
Accurate figures are difficult to obtain, but it's thought that about
6 million Tibetans and 6 million Han live in the area as a whole.
In the larger towns they live cheek by jowl, albeit often in different neighborhoods, although in the rural areas the Tibetans
remain a majority.

The state believes it can handle the divisions between the
ethnicities, as long as those within the Han are smoothed over.
These divides may pose the greatest threat to the prospects of
long-term prosperity and unity in China. The threat is taken
seriously by the Communist Party. It has learned the lessons of
history and knows what happens when the state is weakened by
a fragmented population.

In the nineteenth century, China saw a major reversal in its
trading patterns. Land trade routes through Central Asia had
always been the economic priority, but now sea-lanes became

primary. This reversal was not entirely by choice—the British and other foreign powers had used their military strength to force unfavorable trading terms upon China. As a result, the focus of trade shifted to China's Pacific coast, which helped the communities in that region to develop, but it weakened the trading prospects of the interior, which in turn reduced the amount of money spent on its infrastructure. So while the coastal regions prospered, the dirt-poor farmers remained dirt-poor—and the foreigners became increasingly powerful. This undermined the central authority over the regions and was partly responsible for the splintering of the state. Given such a divided population, the center could not hold. A now thoroughly weakened China was helpless in the face of, first, the "barbarian" colonialists, then civil war, and finally invasion by the old enemy Japan, beginning in 1931.

After World War II, when the Communists had won the civil war, they knew they had to somehow bring the country back together. Communist regimes are not known for their liberal tendencies or their relaxed approach to rules and power sharing. Out went the foreigners and into the regional capitals went the Party cadres. Under Mao they brutally repressed any signs of dissent from the regions and centralized all power in the Party, based in Beijing, which from 1949 was again the capital of the country.

Many of the trade links with the developed world were cut, which partially resulted in that great Communist ideal—equality. Slowly the coastal areas became almost as poor as the interior, solving that imbalance between the regions. Aside from many of the Party bosses, most people continued to be poor for several decades as Mao consolidated power and brought the non-Han territories under his control.

Mao may have reunited the country, but it came at the cost of development, and at exactly the time when other nations in the region were emerging into the world economy and rapidly improving themselves. Japan, South Korea, Singapore, and others were all outpacing China economically, and some militarily as well. If this trend continued, it would threaten both China's defensive security and its internal cohesion, once it became apparent to all how far behind the Chinese had fallen.

Mao's successor, Deng Xiaoping, took a deep breath and a gamble: if Chinese consumers were too poor to buy many of the goods China could produce, the economy had to be opened up to the outside world once more. This meant trading via the Pacific coast, so the coastal regions would again prosper more quickly than the interior, thus risking a repeat of the divisions of the nineteenth and twentieth centuries.

It was, and still is, a race against the clock. The strategy also relies on the economy's maintaining its relentless pace. China has to continue making things. The world has to keep buying these things. If demand drops, China cannot afford, as a normal capitalist system might, to stop making these things. It must keep up production, keep the factories open, subsidize the banks; no matter the surplus—try to dump some abroad at fire-sale prices, sell even more to the part of the domestic population that can afford them. Just don't let the system stop because, if it does, so might the entire country.

This is a fascinating capitalist version of the old Soviet Communist system, which produced as many tractors as the government told it to, regardless of how many were needed. It has lifted hundreds of millions of Chinese out of poverty—at the cost, however, of environmental damage and the renewed widening of the gap between the coastal region and the interior, the rich and poor.

The wage difference between rural and urban workers has narrowed slightly in the past few years, but even now someone in a city can expect to earn three times as much as a country worker. Levels of income inequality in China are among the highest in the world, leading to a feeling that China's wealth-making machine has served the few, not the many—or in Chinese slang, it has served "the Zhao family," an idiom similar to "the top dogs." The expression has its popular roots in a 1920s novel, *The True Story of Ah Q* by Lu Xun, which includes the line "You think you're worthy of the surname Zhao?," referring to a wealthy clan. The phrase began to appear on the Chinese internet in 2015, and now the saying "Zhao and not Zhao" is equivalent to "the haves and have-nots."

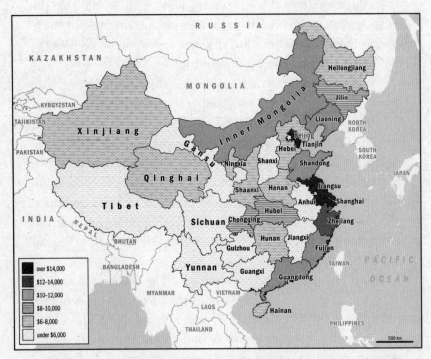

Distribution of wealth across China's provinces, GDP per person (2010).

All countries have wealth inequality, and all have similar sayings, but the difference in China is the size of that gap, and the sheer number of people on the wrong side of it. A 2015 report from the China Family Panel Studies at Peking University exploring the "well-being of the Chinese population" concluded that, overall, wealth inequality was getting worse. It reported that a third of China's wealth is owned by 1 percent of households, while the bottom 25 percent of households account for just 1 percent of wealth. The disparity can be traced back to the opening up of the economy in 1979.

The government is aware of the problems and dangers such division can pose, especially as an internet poll conducted in 2015 suggested that wealth inequality, with its effects on health and education, is the top issue that people want the government to address. In a news item on the report the *People's Daily* newspaper commented, "These inequalities are growing steadily. If they cannot be effectively solved, they may very likely threaten social stability and thus become a bottleneck in future social development."

Even the generations are divided, with some elderly people harking back to the days of Mao and "equality." They look askance at the younger generation, more of whom are urban, better-educated, and consumerist, or at least seek to be. The Communist Party's future is dependent on what it delivers to them and vice versa.

The developing fissures in Chinese society cannot be allowed to widen. One way the government intends to address the problem is to create a much bigger urban consumerist population, thereby offsetting the blows to the economy when exports abroad falter. Estimates vary, but at least 150 million people have left the rural areas this century, and the number is expected to increase. The younger generations move from the countryside, and within them are a disproportionate number of men—married men will sometimes travel to find work in the cities, leaving behind family members to maintain the fields. Despite this, it is crucial to remember that even now about 900 million Chinese live in rural areas and about 500 million in an urban environment.

Change has been quick and will quicken. By 2026 Beijing hopes to have moved another 250 million people, meaning that by then half the population will be urban. This involves a mass uprooting of people, along with the destruction of villages and the building of cities, megacities, roads, and high-speed railways. The majority of the movement continues to be from west to east, the west still tending to be more rural, with higher illiteracy rates; the east, especially toward the seaboard, is increasingly urban and oriented toward technology, industry, and business.

However, the mass migration to the cities reveals and exacerbates another gap within the urban population, again between rich and poor, created by the *hukou* system. This form of registration is rooted in the social structure of the country and has helped to entrench the perception of the rural population as second-class citizens.

The *hukou* system predates the Great Wall, going all the way back to the Xia dynasty (2070–1600 BCE), which started registering every member of every family. In 1953 the Communist Party continued to use the ancient system, but also started to classify people as rural or urban dwellers. This was not just another way to keep tabs on everyone; it was intended to stop people from migrating to urban areas, which could not absorb the influx, and to avoid a repeat of the inequalities between country and city of the previous century.

The system still exists, and everyone's name, parents' names, date of birth, spouse, etc., must be registered—which is normal in many countries. But in China, where you are registered determines where you live and, crucially, where you can receive state aid and in what form. The key divisions arise in the local versus nonlocal and agricultural versus nonagricultural categories.

Let's say your family is registered as nonagricultural Shanghai. This immediately gives you access to a wide range of health and education services in the city. For example, according to a paper in the *China Economic Review*, funding per pupil in Beijing in 1998 was twelve times greater than in Guizhou Province, a ratio that increased to fifteen in 2001. On the other hand, if your family is registered as agricultural in a farming region a thousand miles west of Shanghai, the schools you have access to are way below the standard of those in Shanghai, as are the range of social services. Moreover, your work consists of backbreaking labor, which sometimes results only in a subsistence living.

So, you move to Shanghai to seek work in a factory. Your wages will immediately be higher, and you may be able to send some money back home. But you are registered as "rural agricultural," so you do not qualify for social security or health care in Shanghai. If you marry and have a child, your child is also not registered to be educated in Shanghai. This has resulted in a massive urban underclass of migrant workers from rural areas who are completely cut off from social services. They were second-class citizens in the countryside, and now find that they are regarded as such in the cities too.

The government faces a quandary when trying to address this problem. One option is to initiate a revolution in social funding in the countryside and bring the rural areas up to the standards of the cities. But not only would that cost vast sums of money, it might also keep people in the countryside when the government knows it still needs to create an urban consumer population if its economic policy is to work. Worse still, some of those already in the cities might choose to go home. If that happens, the economic miracle goes bust, unemployment rockets, and social disorder follows.

Somehow Beijing needs to balance the books. It must fund a *hukou* system in the cities for those who have come from the rural areas, while also increasing the funding for social services in general as the cities continue to grow—then somehow, ideally simultaneously, raise standards in the countryside while still encouraging movement to the built-up areas, preferably creating new cities in the interior.

This is quite a challenge, and how to tackle it is not straight-forward; quite apart from the vast expense, the creation of so many new urban environments, spread out around the country, is a logistical challenge. Beijing is toying with the idea of allowing regional governments more power to tax locally, to raise revenues through land sales, and to spend the proceeds as they see fit. It might work. But if it fails, Beijing will have to bail out the local governments. And even if it succeeds, it might fuel what the Party dreads—regionalism.

Deng appears to have known that his gamble would give rise to many of these issues. In a famous interview in 1986, Mike Wallace of CBS News asked the then eighty-two-year-old Communist leader about the startling phrase attributed to him from the late 1970s that "to get rich is glorious." Deng replied, "According to Marxism, Communist society is based on material abundance. . . . So to get rich is no sin. However, what we mean by getting rich is different from what you mean. Wealth in a socialist society belongs to the people. To get rich in a socialist society means prosperity for the entire people. The principles of socialism are, first, development of production, and, second, common prosperity. We permit some people and some regions to become prosperous first, for the purpose of achieving common prosperity faster. That is why our policy will not lead to polarization, to a situation where the rich get richer while the poor get poorer."

He was half wrong and half right, because the rich have gotten richer. However, although the poor have not gotten poorer, in relative terms they are less well-off because of the massive and increasing gap in wealth equality that has emerged.

China has created a middle class of about 400 million people and lifted hundreds of millions more out of abject poverty. It's a work in progress, and you can't rule out the possibility of things going backward, but enough Chinese still remember just how poor most people were before, with almost no chance of lifting themselves out of that poverty—after all, most of the grandparents of today's mature adults were peasants in a feudal society. This buys the Party a little more time to address the problem; but if it cannot soon narrow the wealth gap, eventually the resentment from the "not Zhao" will grow.

Another problem the government faces is an aging population. This isn't unique to China. But it is a particular issue for China because of the one-child policy, which means that the population is aging much faster than in other countries. In less than a decade the number of elderly will rise from 200 million to 300 million. Is the government prepared for such a change in demographics? Its economic policy has been reliant on a young and plentiful labor force. Proportionally, this pool of available laborers—and taxpayers—will get smaller at the same time as the financial burden of providing care to the aging population increases, putting economic progress at risk.

Again the solution is not clear. One option is to raise the retirement age by five years, but that simply postpones the problem and creates another: the college graduates the education system is churning out want jobs; unemployment and lack of promotion are already difficulties and will only be exacerbated if the older generation retires later. The alternative is to ensure that the social services can provide pensions and to drop the one-child policy. The latter was done in 2015, but the government is still looking for ways to fund the former.

These multiple divisions simmer within the Han population, all of which pose a potential threat to the government if they worsen. The authorities must retain control of China's heartland if they are to keep its economic policy on track and the outlying regions in check. Their solution is to control the flow of information, to prevent dissenting ideas from spreading, to stop opposition from consolidating. They must divide in order to unite; and so, in the age of the internet, the Great Firewall of China came into being.

This creates contradictory policies: suppressing information while simultaneously creating a vibrant economy that is increasingly based on data exchange across the country and with the outside world. In the early days of the internet this was not a problem for a government hell-bent on protecting its position as China's only source of power and information. Access was limited, so all internal mass communication was state controlled, and the few internet cafés or universities connected to the Web could be easily monitored, both physically and electronically. As late as 2005, only 10 percent of the population had access to the internet. Now, however, the figure is 50 percent—and rising. That's about 700 million users, which is roughly a quarter of the world's online population. And that is harder to control.

Keeping the Chinese people digitally cut off from the outside world has been easier than dividing them from each other. What the outside world calls the Great Firewall is known in China as the Golden Shield. This outward-facing firewall is supposed to protect the Chinese population from such damaging ideas as democracy, free speech, and unplugged culture. Despite some work-arounds such as virtual private network (VPN) services, which are designed to tunnel under the wall, most Chinese people do not have access to sites as diverse as *Time*, Dropbox, the *Economist*, Facebook, YouTube, Amnesty International, the *Tibet Post*, the Norwegian Broadcasting Company, *Le Monde*, or Pornhub.

The inner walls are to prevent potentially political cyber networks from emerging and to keep what is happening in one part of the country, for example, Xinjiang, quiet from the rest. The Party particularly fears social media's being used to organize like-minded groups who might then gather in public places to demonstrate, which could in turn lead to rioting.

Rogier Creemers, professor of law and governance at Leiden University in the Netherlands, is one of the world's leading experts on the Chinese internet. He argues that the outside world doesn't fully understand the Chinese government's attitude to the digital revolution: "I would say that in comparison we generally see the internet through a rose-tinted lens, that everyone's free, there's freedom of information, democracy, etc. China from the get-go was a lot more skeptical. They thought new technology would have new consequences and we need to deal with those consequences. When the Chinese talk about *wangluo anquan*—cyber security—they don't just mean technological integrity [protecting the physical system, e.g., power lines, from damage] or cyber-crime. They mean the entire role internet technology may have in destabilizing economic and social stability. So, things we may not see as cyber security such as, say, online rumors, they do."

China has its own versions of companies such as Google, Facebook, and Twitter in the shape of Baidu, Renren, and Weibo, but they are heavily monitored. The level of censorship varies between the regions; for example, in Tibet and Xinjiang the firewalls are both higher and deeper. A university student in Shanghai might get away with using a VPN to access a banned foreign news source, but one in the Uighur capital of Ürümqi would probably receive an invitation to discuss the technology at the city police HQ. Who is using VPNs, and for what reason, can be traced, and the state wants to know all about it. It knows that some domestic and foreign companies, and indeed some individuals, will use the technology for business purposes, to which it largely turns a blind eye. But in 2009 Uighur activists gained access to Facebook, and the company's continuing legal troubles in China can be traced back to that incident.

Until 2013 a succession of start-up media platforms saw the business opportunities the internet offered and some became quite popular but ended up in hot water and were banned. In August

2015, for example, the start-up news site Initium Media launched from Hong Kong. Just a week later, after an explosion in a chemical factory in the northern city of Tianjin, Initium's reporters got past the security cordons. They discovered that 173 people had died and followed up by reporting on the factory owner's high-level connections. Days later, with no official announcement, the site was blocked in mainland China, forcing the company to change its business model and concentrate on reaching Chinese people outside China—a somewhat smaller market.

The authorities were particularly alarmed in 2010 when smartphones became available and affordable, and people could spread information easily and quickly, 24-7. So, as Professor Creemers explains, the leadership used a number of policies and regulations to push social media into the private sphere: "For example it has tried to ensure that the Weibo [microblogging] platform has become less popular, but that WeChat is widely promoted. Why? Because WeChat is not public: if you share something within your chat group, it is not shared by massive numbers of people, and what is shared is shared slowly. This makes it easier to monitor—it's divide and rule."

The new Chinese cyber-security legislation, which came into law in 2017, has built the walls higher than ever, metaphorically speaking. The legislation, formulated to ensure "digital sovereignty," includes classic catchall laws designed to mean what the Party interprets them to mean. For example, if a foreign company is involved in any part of China's critical information structure, it must store all of its information on physical databases inside China. What constitutes "critical" has not been defined. This information can be accessed by the government and cannot be sent outside China without being checked by the intelligence services. Foreign and domestic social media companies must keep all registration details by would-be users, then track and record their online activity for at least six months and be prepared to hand over that data if the government demands it. The legal language is so loose that, theoretically, any foreign company that has offices in China could be required to store within China any information it has about a Chinese citizen. A company must also agree to actively assist any investigation into its data storage by the government.

All this costs money, which the domestic companies would rather be spending on other things and which foreign companies might balk at. With the added worry about the risk to their intellectual property, IT and new-technology firms especially might decide to invest in a more benign business environment instead. While this could in theory free up space for domestic companies to develop, they are in turn hampered by the restrictions on the free flow of information and ideas. Even before the legislation, in 2016, the *Washington Post* reported that, according to the American Chamber of Commerce in China, four out of five of its member companies had experienced a negative impact on business due to internet regulations and censorship.

Professor Creemers describes the Party as "the ultimate risk-management company," constantly scanning the horizon for any signs of political unrest. He believes that when the internet first came to China, the authorities took a few years to work out how to deal with it, but now they are clear where to focus their efforts: "The most important tactic the government has developed is in forestalling organized opposition. They will not allow crosscutting interest to materialize. They believe they must keep people divided so that they can't organize along lines of class, geography, or whatever. The traditional media were organized so that they were limited; for example, professional newspapers for the steel industry, which would only write about steel, provincial papers could only report about their region. So even if one outlet went rogue, there was limited damage. The internet spoiled that model. For the first time in recent history individual Chinese people have access to the tools of mass communication, and there were a few years where the internet ran amok. Some people think the government is paranoid; I'm not so sure, I think they are very soberly aware of everything."

Aware of the growing risks to his monopoly on power, President Xi has personally led the push to overhaul China's cyber strategy by ordering the groups crafting it to report directly to him. For the president, the propagation of communication is a potential threat, so the censorship starts at the top.

Xi is the first Chinese leader to come to power fully aware of the potential of the internet. Since assuming office in 2013, he has personally overseen all of China's cyber strategies, both internal and external. All the major government cyber departments report directly to a committee he chairs. He has used this power not only to devise the policies, but also to help create something of a cult of personality around him. The Party has even "bestowed" upon him the title of Core Leader, which puts him in a pantheon occupied only by Mao and Deng and indicates something close to absolute power. The Core Leader's face is now everywhere in China, gazing down on you from billboards, in offices, and on millions of products on sale in tourist shops across the country, from Beijing and Shanghai to the Great Wall.

At the 19th National Congress of the Communist Party in late 2017 the president further consolidated power. He ensured his supporters were elected to the Politburo, and they in turn now promote the concept of "Xi Jinping Thought on Socialism with Chinese Characteristics for a New Era." This was the first time since Mao that a leader's ideas were promoted as "thought," which in Chinese political terms is the top of the tree.

Yet another digital divide is between the minority of Chinese who speak English and those who do not. Type *Tiananmen Square, uprising, tank* into Baidu's search box in German and you might possibly get back a link, in German, to the events of 1989. Type the same words in Chinese and you'll probably see "According to relevant laws, regulations, and policies, some results are not displayed," or, if you're lucky, a nice photomontage of one of the great tourist attractions of the world.

David Bandurski, a writer at the China Media Project, has noted the introduction of a new term by the Cyberspace Administration of China—*positive energy*. This, he argues, is a euphemism for content that is acceptable to the authorities, but some Chinese scholars are "concerned about the possibility of a crackdown on 'rightists' under the guise of promoting 'positive energy.'" Until 2016, the head of the administration was Lu Wei, who understands the power of information. Lu had worked his way up through the ranks of the Xinhua News Agency before taking up his cyber role. He was then promoted to deputy director of the Publicity Department of the Communist Party of China, which in essence means deputy head of all media control in the country. Lu said his country had "cyber governance with Chinese characteristics," echoing Deng's phrase "socialism with Chinese characteristics." Lu added that his country was "very hospitable to the outside world, but I can choose who will be a guest in my home."

Internet censorship does restrict China's economic potential. The country is still the world's leader in e-commerce, with digital retail sales making up almost 40 percent of the global total, but retail internet sales and innovation are two different things. China wants not only to create a much bigger internal market but also to make high-end goods and develop cutting-edge technology. It is very aware that although iPhones are made in China, their design and technology come from far away in Silicon Valley.

The government believes this is a price worth paying for the time being; it is part of the balancing act and gamble with time. The Communist Party needs to ensure it can feed 1.4 billion people, find work for them, find things for them to make, and find markets to which they can sell those things. At the same time, it believes it must also crush the possibility of any organized opposition, be that democracy-loving students, independence-minded Tibetans, Falun Gong–practicing religious types, or even artistic expressions of freedom. If that means holding back the free flow of information at the expense of the economic miracle—so be it.

Qin Shi Huang knocked down the internal walls of the warring states only once he was confident in his ability to hold them together. More than two thousand years later, the power of the leadership, and the unity of the Han and the nation, still come first. Even if that unity is achieved through a digital wall that separates China from the rest of the world and divides itself.

CHAPTER 2

USA

Show me a fifty-foot wall and I'll show you a fifty-one-foot ladder.

—Janet Napolitano,
former US secretary of
Homeland Security

Previous pages: Part of the existing border barrier along the US-Mexico border, separating Ciudad Juárez, Mexico, from Sunland Park, New Mexico.

On the day after Donald Trump was elected the forty-fifth president of the United States, the über-arch, neoconservative commentator Ann Coulter published a meticulously planned "detailed schedule" of the priorities for his first one hundred days in office. She began with "Day 1: start building the wall." Then progressed to "Day 2: continue building the wall. Day 3: continue building the wall. Day 4: continue building the wall." This went on until "Day 100: report to American people about progress of wall. Keep building the wall." It's all good knockabout stuff, based on hubris and clickbait journalism, and it helps pay her mortgage, but it's unlikely Ms. Coulter was stupid enough to think it would happen. And of course, it didn't.

For months, Mr. Trump had been promising to build a wall on the US-Mexico border to help curb illegal immigration into the USA. Though he appears mostly to "consult his own genius" (to use the French phrase about President Valéry Giscard d'Estaing), even before he entered the White House he was informed of the expense of wall building, the political opposition to it, and, of equal importance, the terrain upon which the wall was to be built. Speeches about "a wall, a great big beautiful wall" played well with his core support, but that is a poor basis on which to found a massive engineering project, and the plans in his head soon ran into a wall of reality—and the quicksand of Washington, DC.

Within weeks of Trump's election, conservative Republican senators such as Lindsey Graham were scrambling out of that quicksand. Mr. Graham, one of the smartest operators on Capitol

Hill, began talking about the word *wall* being a "code word for better border security," as if the president's speeches had been delivered in the style of the secret BBC radio broadcasts to the French Resistance—"This is London! Jean has a long mustache."

It had not been a code word; Mr. Trump had even specified that the wall would be built of precast concrete planks with an average height of thirty feet. However, pretending that it was a metaphorical term was a useful linguistic trick by which to enable the Grand Old Party to carry on without too much damage. President Trump went on to sign a $1.1 trillion bill to fund government spending for the rest of the fiscal year. The money set aside for the wall totaled zero.

This is perhaps the most famous nonexistent wall in the world. But even though it is yet to be constructed, it is a powerful symbol of how division has driven and continues to drive the cultural and political juggernaut that is the USA.

Still, a lack of funding wasn't going to stop the president. The US Customs and Border Protection agency invited bids to build Trump's wall, with the stipulation that the barrier be strong enough to withstand blows for up to four hours from "sledgehammers, car jacks, pickaxes . . . propane or butane or other similar hand-held tools." Other rules were that it must be "physically imposing in height" and "impossible to climb." The resulting two hundred or so submissions were interesting.

One entry was from a Rod Hadrian of California, who nonchalantly brushed past the limited success his namesake had had in keeping out the alien hordes. Another, from Pittsburgh-based Clayton Industries, said it had the answer—a chain-link fence on the Mexican side of the border, and a wall on the American side. In between them would run a trench filled with nuclear waste. From Clarence, Illinois, Crisis Resolution Security Services entered a Great Wall of China look-alike, complete with turrets and crenellated walls. Its two twenty-six-foot concrete walls were built on a thirty-foot packed-earth berm. Along the top would run a pedestrian walkway, as on the Great Wall of China, but the company's founder, Michael Hari, also saw the potential for cycling along the wall and turning it into a tourist attraction. Mr. Hari, a former sheriff's deputy, claimed to have compassion for people who try to enter the USA illegally, but said he submitted his design for patriotic reasons, telling the *Chicago Tribune*, "We would look at the wall as not just a physical barrier to immigration but also as a symbol of the American determination to defend our culture, our language, our heritage, from any outsiders."

This is the heart of the matter. Walls can reduce illegal crossings, although the US-Mexico border barrier is especially porous, but they do more—they make people who "want something to be done" feel that something is being done. As Dr. Reece Jones of the University of Hawaii, and author of *Violent Borders*, says, "Walls rarely work, but they are powerful symbols of action against perceived problems." The Great Wall of China aimed to separate the civilized world from the barbarians; Trump's wall aims to separate Americans from non-Americans. It's the concept of the nation that unites Americans—and now, for some, Trump's wall signifies the preservation and sanctity of that concept. It endorses the idea of Making America Great Again and symbolizes the support that exists for putting America First.

All countries contain divisions. The founding fathers knew this and attempted to establish one nation under God, with equality for all. The flaws in the early days, notably slavery, are well known, but after a troubled history the USA has become, in constitutional and legal terms, a free country, protecting the rights and equality of its citizens and striving to break down the internal divides. This is a remarkable feat: equality in law is a strong basis for achieving equality in practice.

One of the USA's ideals has been that all its citizens are defined as being American, a population bound by shared values, not by race, religion, or ethnic background. The motto held in the beak of the eagle in the Great Seal of the United States reads *E pluribus unum* (out of many, one). More than most countries, the USA has partially succeeded in blending peoples from all over the world into a nation. In Lebanon or Syria, for example, national identity falls well behind ethnic, religious, or tribal identity. Nevertheless, you don't have to look too closely at the "shining city on a hill" to see that some parts of it are far from lustrous and others are showing rust.

Each wall tells its own story. The Saudi barrier along the Iraqi border is functional, and it functions. It does not stand as a testament to Saudi suspicion of "the other" because across that border the "others" are mostly of the same religion, language, and culture as the people in the kingdom. America is different. It's the "otherness" of those who are entering the country, and the fear that they could dilute what some perceive to be "American" culture, that makes the wall so important to its supporters. For those who oppose it, the wall goes against American values of freedom, liberty, equality, and an America for all. The controversy about the wall gets to the heart of the debate about who gets to define what "American" means in the coming century.

According to the US Census Bureau, in 2015 some 27.5 million people lived in Texas, of whom 38.8 percent were Hispanic. Studies by the Pew Research Center, a nonpartisan think tank, suggest that in 2014 the state had 4.5 million immigrants, the majority of them Spanish speaking. This trend is also seen in some of the other states in the region. Head south from Phoenix, Arizona, through the flat desert lands, toward the border about 180 miles away: the farther south you go, the more Spanish you hear spoken, and the more Hispanic life becomes. As this trend grows, within a few decades several states might give Spanish legal equality with English as an official language in schools and government. At the federal level the USA has no official language, but in thirty of the fifty states it is currently listed as English. However, some states, including Texas and New Mexico, already use both English and Spanish in government documents, and more will inevitably follow suit as the years pass. As the Spanish language and culture become increasingly dominant, some regions may start calling for even greater autonomy from the federal system. This may be decades down the line, but it is a real possibility; history is littered with examples of nation-states evolving in such a way.

So some parts of the American electorate are concerned that the United States will no longer be a white-majority, English-speaking country as its demographics change, and this is one issue driving current US politics. Nativism seems to have reached a peak with the election of Trump, and the erection of a concrete wall would symbolize a particular period in American history. But it's important to understand that the US-Mexico border has long been troublesome. Its current route was mapped out following the 1848 Treaty of Guadalupe Hidalgo, which ended the Mexican-American War. But its location before that had been quite different.

Where exactly the dividing line lay became an issue of national security after the Louisiana Purchase of 1803, bringing the Mississippi River system, which flowed into the crucial port of New Orleans, into the United States. At the time, the Spanish controlled Texas as part of "New Spain," which now became a concern for the Americans as it meant that a potentially hostile military force could approach within striking range of New Orleans. Americans wanted control of the region and claimed that Texas was part of the Louisiana Purchase. Spain begged to differ but was in a weak position from the start. According to a Spanish census of 1793, Texas had fewer than five thousand non–Native American settlers.

Spain was far away, the European wars had left it weakened, and the USA was next door to Texas, with ambitions to expand.

In 1819, as part of the ensuing negotiations, the two countries agreed that Florida would go to the USA and Spain would continue to control Texas, with the United States giving up any claim to the area. However, in 1821 Mexico won independence from Spain and claimed Texas as part of its territory. In Texas, the Spanish-speaking population still greatly outnumbered the non–Native American settlers. Mexico felt that the greatest threat to its hegemony there was the Comanche nation, so its priority was to increase the population of settlers to consolidate control—but this actually helped to deliver the opposite outcome.

Thinking that a larger American population would act as a buffer between the Comanche and its own settlers and would easily be absorbed into the population, the Mexican government gave all sorts of inducements to lure colonists from the USA as well as Mexico. Newcomers were offered Mexican citizenship three years after arrival. However, the new immigrants resisted certain aspects of Mexican culture and did not assimilate as the government had hoped. Two obstacles in particular stood in the way: religion and slavery.

Most of the Americans arriving were Protestants, some of them devout. They were not about to embrace Catholicism, which Mexico insisted was to be the territory's sole religion. Many of them were also slave owners, whereas Mexico supported the abolition of slavery, officially outlawing it in 1829. Realizing the problem, Mexico tried to limit immigration, but Americans kept coming illegally and by 1834 outnumbered Mexican settlers by nearly ten to one. The growing hostility well suited Washington, DC, which encouraged an uprising against Mexican rule; Texas declared itself a republic in 1836. It then tried to join the USA, but for several years Washington denied the request, for two main reasons. First, a de facto buffer zone between New Orleans and Mexico had been created, and Washington didn't consider it worthwhile to upset the Mexicans. Second, the United States was in turmoil over slavery, and Texas was a slave state. Nevertheless, by 1845 Washington agreed: Texas became the twenty-eighth state, and the USA's southern border now reached the Rio Grande.

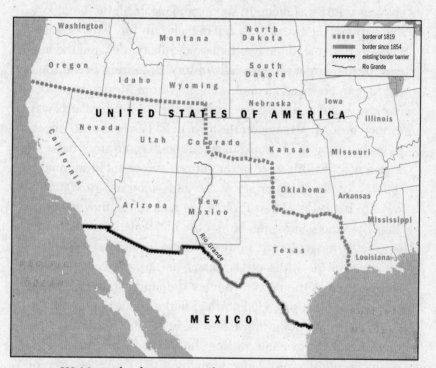

US-Mexico border in 1819 and in 2017, with existing fencing.

The USA then pushed on ever westward, sparking the Mexican-American War. In 1846 a skirmish along the Rio Grande lit the fuse. The war lasted until 1848, and when it ended, Mexico lost about a third of its territory in the Treaty of Guadalupe Hidalgo, including nearly all of present-day New Mexico, Arizona, Nevada, Utah, and California. And that was that. Mexico was weak, America was strong. But this situation will not necessarily last forever. The borders have changed before and could do so again. The Americans are aware of that: they've been barricading themselves in along their southern border for a long time, and this is not solely a Republican trait.

Following the end of the Mexican-American War in 1848, a six-year effort was made to survey and establish the boundary line between the two nations, but initially only fifty-two boundary markers designated the two-thousand-mile border, and the line was, by and large, only casually observed. During Prohibition (1920–33), however, alcohol smuggling from Mexico markedly increased, and to combat the problem the US Border Patrol was formed in 1924. A year later the town of El Paso was encouraged to build a "hog-tight, horse-high and bootlegger-proof barbed-wire fence." Efforts were never entirely successful in stemming the flow of illegal liquor across the line—after all, great profits were to be made. When Prohibition ended, the movement of illegal products across the border did not. Americans started to consume ever-greater quantities of drugs, so instead of alcohol, ever-greater quantities of marijuana, heroin, and cocaine were shipped across the border to meet demand, while increasing numbers of people headed north to find work.

One turning point in the flow of migrants from Mexico to the United States came during the Great Depression. With serious economic problems throughout the USA, the issue of immigrants taking American jobs became key, and Mexicans were targeted in particular—during the Mexican Repatriation, somewhere between five hundred thousand and 2 million people were deported to Mexico, many of whom were actually US-born citizens. The USA changed its strategy once it joined World War II; with the majority of American laborers absorbed into the wartime economy, from 1942 a concerted effort was made to attract workers, particularly for farming industries, and later, to service a booming postwar America, a trend that continued until the mid-1960s.

Government policy toward immigration changed again as economic downturn and increased migration saw renewed calls for immigration measures, and the barriers started to go up in earnest. In 1978 the Immigration and Naturalization Service (INS) put out bids for two twelve-foot-high fences topped with barbed wire to be built in Texas. A contractor from Houston reassured the INS that his designs would "sever the toes of anyone trying to scale" them given the sharpness of the razor wire he would supply. Fence building had already increased, but this statement attracted national attention and outrage, with critics dubbing the scheme the Tortilla Curtain. This incident raised awareness further in the national consciousness—and it's been rising ever since.

The fence building continued, albeit with less celebration of finger- and toe-severing, but levels of immigration did not noticeably decrease. In 1986 President Ronald Reagan made a deal: around 3 million unauthorized immigrants who had been living in the USA since before 1982 were given "amnesty." In return, Congress approved more stringent regulations to prevent companies from hiring illegal immigrants, as well as tightened border security.

Over the following years, additional barriers were built, but on a limited budget and on occasion using leftover materials from the Vietnam War, such as metal sheets known as perforated steel planking, which had been used as temporary aircraft-landing strips. A stretch of wall in Southern California was built using tens of thousands of these metal sheets, but to cut costs they were erected horizontally instead of vertically. They covered more ground, but the barrier was thus lower, and as the sheets were corrugated, they also provided handy toeholds for anyone wanting a bit of assistance in climbing over them. No matter what fences went up, people could still overcome them relatively easily. The Border Patrol officers began to think of the various barriers simply as a way to reduce the speed at which people could enter the USA, therefore making it easier to catch them, but not as a means to stop them from entering.

In the early 2000s, with George Bush in office and in the wake of 9/11, the US government launched a full border fortification program, imposing an unprecedented degree of separation along most of the boundary. Congress approved the Secure Fence Act, agreeing that another seven hundred miles could be built—among those voting for the measure were Hillary Clinton and Barack Obama; but even after these improvements and with cross-party support, the fence was, as Border Patrol spokesman Mike Scioli described it in 2008, little more than "a speed bump in the desert."

When President Obama came to the White House, the barrier was more than six hundred miles, and he kept building—extending the fence, in some regions double-layering it, occasionally even triple-layering. His term in office also saw a significant increase in the number of forced removals of illegal immigrants compared to the Bush years. This should not come as too much of a surprise given his speech to the Senate in April 2006 when he described the immigration system as "broken," allowing a "flood of illegals" into America:

> The American people are a welcoming and generous people. But those who enter our country illegally, and those who employ them, disrespect the rule of law. And because we live in an age where terrorists are challenging our borders, we simply cannot allow people to pour into the United States undetected, undocumented, and unchecked. Americans are right to demand better border security and better enforcement of the immigration

laws. . . . And before any guest worker is hired, the job must be made available to Americans at a decent wage with benefits.

Obama adopted a softer tone when he called for undocumented immigrants to be allowed to come out of the shadows and "step on a path toward full participation in our society . . . not just for humanitarian reasons; not just because these people, having broken the law, did so for the best of motives, to try and provide a better life for their children; but also because this is the only practical way we can get a handle on the population that is within our borders right now." This pragmatic approach to the problem recognized the difficulties of identifying and deporting these immigrants and made room for them to stay, but accepted that illegal immigration was a problem and took steps to stop the "flood."

However, the success of all the attempts by Obama and his predecessors to erect barriers along the border to stem the flow of immigrants is questionable. The unauthorized migrant population did fall from 12.4 million in 2007 to 11.1 million in 2011. However, it is difficult to pinpoint what percentage can be attributed to the barriers, to increased deportations, or to changing economic conditions.

Part of the problem is that the USA still offers opportunities—not just for those looking for employment but also for unscrupulous employers willing to exploit their workers. Here we face one aspect of the hypocrisy behind some of the anti-immigrant arguments. Countless American companies, big and small, employ huge numbers of illegal immigrants, pay them little, give them no legal rights, and hide their presence from the authorities. The government could begin to arrest lots of American management teams that knowingly hire illegal immigrants. How popular this would be with companies that rely on cheap labor for construction contracts and fruit picking is another matter.

Ultimately, few barriers are impenetrable. People are resourceful, and those desperate enough will find a way around, under, or over them. Extra barriers simply push would-be illegal immigrants farther and farther into unguarded, unpopulated areas. These are often in the desert and usually have to be crossed on foot, meaning that thousands of people die from exposure as they attempt to make it to the promised land.

There's an irony in building something that might seem to solve a problem—stopping people from getting in—but simultaneously stops them from getting out. Many people enter the United States legally, on a tourist visa. In the present decade, more than half those crossing south to north have stayed on; however, a functioning wall makes it harder for them to go home once they have become an illegal. If you're working illegally in, say, Phoenix, even if things aren't going well for you, there's little incentive in trying to leave when you know that you may well be arrested on the way out.

Another irony here is that Mexico has its own strict immigration laws and annually deports more people than does the USA. Its immigration policy features racial overtones and is underpinned by the 1974 General Law of Population, which stipulates that people hoping to come to Mexico can be turned away if their presence upsets "the equilibrium of the national demographics." America's laws are tough on foreigners, but Mexico's are tougher. For example, if you are caught in Mexico without authorization for a second time, you can face up to ten years in jail. Republican politicians in the United States delight in reminding their Mexican counterparts of these laws. Some tease them by suggesting that all three countries that are part of the North American Free Trade Agreement (NAFTA) have the same immigration laws but base them on those of Mexico.

America's immigration policies have also been influenced by the rise of terrorist incidents in the USA and across the Western world. Trump has responded with a harsher stance on immigration than his predecessors, with travel bans, the wall, and a determination to deport and deter. Whether any of this helps, particularly the wall, is debatable. There isn't any evidence that terrorists have entered the USA across the border with Mexico— the Department of Homeland Security has made several statements that contradict claims of threats from south of the border; for example, in 2014 it said that it had "no credible intelligence to suggest terrorist organizations are actively plotting to cross the south-west border."

Little intelligence (in the public domain, at least) indicates much of a threat in allowing refugees into the country. Alex Nowrasteh, an immigration expert at the Cato Institute, a libertarian think tank in Washington, DC, researched terror attacks in the USA going back four decades and concluded that of the 3.25 million refugees allowed in during that period, only twenty had been convicted of attempting or committing terrorism on US soil, and "only three Americans have been killed in attacks committed by refugees—all by Cuban refugees in the 1970s." Since 9/11, over 80 percent of those involved in terrorist incidents have been citizens or legal residents of the USA.

Bill Clinton pointed out that the spread of ideas could not be stopped by walls, using as an example the 2015 terrorist incident in San Bernardino, California, in which fourteen people were killed and another twenty-two wounded. The attack was carried out by Syed Rizwan Farook and Tashfeen Malik, who had both been converted to radical Islam via social media—Farook was born in the USA and Malik was a lawful permanent resident. President Clinton commented, "You can build a wall across our border with Canada as well. Create giant sea walls along the Atlantic and the Pacific. . . . We can send the whole US Navy to the Gulf Coast and keep anybody from getting in there. We could use every airplane the US Air Force has got in the air to stop planes from landing. You still couldn't keep out the social media." He did have a point, but President Trump was unswayed by the advice of his predecessor. Arguing that social media is difficult to police, or that terrorists do not enter the United States illegally across the Mexican border, has less emotional resonance with many people than the benefits of a physical wall.

What do continue to flow across the border are illegal products—and this is a two-way street. Drugs made in Mexico can sell for many times their production costs because millions of Americans will pay top dollar for their illegal substance of choice. Going the other way, guns bought legally in the USA can be sold in Mexico for a huge markup. Evidence suggests that barriers do little to interfere with these trades, and that more drugs cross via official checkpoints than come through the desert—it's cheaper for drug runners to bribe an official than to organize a run through the patrolled borderlands or to dig a tunnel. That is why the gang bosses fight one another for control of the walled-off border towns. Win the town and you win access to the officials. Gun and drug smugglers are often cold-blooded murderous thugs, but they are also businessmen.

It would make sense for the two countries to work together on this issue, not just to control movement of people and illegal goods and substances, but to encourage trade and economic prosperity in the region. Mexico and the USA are very different places in language, skin tone, religion, climate, and history, but they are increasingly tied through economics, and if anything can move through, under, around, and over barriers it is the profit motive. While unwanted immigration can be prevented in many ways, a vibrant, booming economy south of the Rio Grande would do more to reduce the northward flow than a wall, as far fewer job seekers would bother to cross.

Take the car industry in the area, which has become known as the Texas-Mexico Automotive SuperCluster Region. Within Texas and four Mexican states near the border are twenty-seven vehicle-assembly plants that rely on one another to produce finished models. Working together, they have established a successful industry on both sides of the border, creating jobs, encouraging innovation, and boosting the local economies. Making sure that arrangements such as these can continue unimpeded is in the best interests of both countries.

Despite this, in the first year of Trump's presidency the USA continued to slowly withdraw into itself, scuttling multilateral trade deals, pushing to renegotiate NAFTA, and casting doubt on America's commitment to NATO. The wisdom of these moves is debatable, but what is not is that only the USA can do this. America constitutes approximately 22 percent of the world's economy. More important, it can pull up the drawbridge because it exports only around 14 percent of its GDP, according to the World Bank, and 40 percent of that goes next door to Mexico and Canada. So even though global trade wars cost America dear, it is the only major power that can absorb the potential losses of withdrawing from globalization without seriously endangering itself in the short term.

However, history suggests that isolationism does harm the USA in the long term; whenever it has withdrawn into itself, it has always been drawn out again, and not always when it was prepared to be. The pros and cons of isolationism are one of many conflicts within American discourse now when the great republic seems to be divided in many ways.

So, will Trump's big, beautiful wall get built?

Guns, *drugs*, *illegals*—these can be emotional terms in political dialogue, and people want solutions to problems. So even after entering the White House, President Trump kept up the bluster, telling the National Rifle Association, "We'll build the wall. Don't even think about it, that's an easy one," and assuring his supporters, "If we have to close down our government, we're building that wall."

The Donald may not be aware of the old English phrase "Fine words butter no parsnips" (nothing is achieved by empty promises or flattery), but it certainly applies here. Despite the pre- and postelection rhetoric, the concept of Trump's wall ran into the problems he had been warned about, the same ones his predecessors had with border control: politics, budget, state law, federal law, nature, and international treaties. For example, Mexico and the USA each have copies of the document they signed in 1970, solemnly swearing to keep the floodplain of the Rio Grande open. President Obama went ahead and built a fence anyway, but the terms of the treaty forced the barrier so far into the USA that it had to be built with huge gaps to allow Americans to get to their houses. This design flaw was soon noticed by Latin Americans looking for ways to illegally enter the Land of the Free.

Private citizens own about two-thirds of US southern-border property and land. Many of them do not want a huge concrete wall in their backyards and can take legal action to stop it from being built. If the state buys the land, the previous owners must receive "just compensation," and deciding what that might be can be a lengthy process. Native American tribes can and have launched legal campaigns as well. For example, the Tohono O'odham Nation owns land that straddles both countries and has gone to court to prevent it from being divided.

The landscape itself presents further obstacles. The border stretches two thousand miles from the Pacific Ocean to the Gulf of Mexico via California, Arizona, New Mexico, and Texas. At most a wall could be built along a thousand miles of it, with natural obstacles such as steep terrain, bedrock, and water getting in the way along the rest of the route.

Even so, the figures being bandied about for the project are so huge they are almost meaningless to most of us. Pick a figure, any figure, then add on a bit because no one's sure how much a wall would cost—other than a lot. Trump has estimated the price tag at between $10 and $12 billion, but most other sources suggest that the figure would be much higher. The Massachusetts Institute of Technology (MIT) has produced an estimate (albeit from quite rough approximations of the cost of materials, labor, and an uncertain time frame) that a thousand miles of thirty-foot-high concrete would cost $27–$40 billion. Other guesses included $25 billion and $21 billion, the latter from Homeland Security. This is still a staggering amount of money, but if you were selling the idea, perhaps you could say it's only $21 million per mile. . . . None of these figures account for maintenance costs. Nevertheless, many people won't be perturbed by the expense—after all, Trump has claimed Mexico will pay for the wall, a suggestion that was greeted enthusiastically by his supporters, though it's a tougher sell south of the border, with former Mexican president Vicente Fox Quesada declaring, "Mexico is not going to pay for that f***ing wall."

A cheaper way forward would be to buy into Senator Graham's face-saving claim that the word *wall* is code for "better security." After all, a fence might partially do the job. In parallel with other measures, it would be much more cost-effective, and it would have the psychological effect of satisfying the need of some voters for a physical barrier to make them feel safer. Politicians are not strangers to the advantages of gestures over practicalities. But, so far, Trump remains firm that a wall is what the people want, and that is what they're going to get. By early 2018 several prototypes of the wall had gone up, but opposition from Congress to funding the project had not gone down.

The obstacles to the construction of the wall are substantial. The legal cases are conceptual roadblocks, which can admittedly sometimes be bypassed; but is it worth it, given the other physical barriers in the way of building it? If the wall is a political statement,

then for its supporters the answer would be yes. The more concrete, the stronger the message, the more the core support swells.
As long as immigration declines (which may well happen, due to
a combination of other security measures or economic factors),
then the gaps in the wall will be overlooked by many voters, and it
will be hailed as a key policy in stopping foreigners from entering
and in protecting American values. A wall is a reassuring physical
symbol—and sometimes symbolism can outweigh practicalities.

Other presidents have fortified the border with Mexico, but
Trump's wall is particularly divisive because of this particular
moment in US history. The politics of building the wall isn't
just about keeping Mexicans out. A border defines a nation,
and Trump's wall is attempting to define what America is—both
physically and ideologically. To understand how it reflects and
deepens historical divides, we need to look at the other fissures
splitting the country.

Of all the divisions in America, race appears to be the widest.
The USA has approximately 324 million people. According to the
CIA World Factbook, based on the 2010 census, of these 72.4
percent are white, 12.6 percent black, 4.8 percent Asian, and just
under 1 percent Amerindian and Alaska Native. People of "two
or more races" comprise 2.9 percent, and Native Hawaiian and
other Pacific Islanders 0.2 percent, with "other" at 6.2 percent.
You will have noticed here the absence of the growing Hispanic
population. This is because the US Census Bureau considers
"Hispanic" to mean someone of Spanish/Hispanic/Latino origin
"who may be any race or ethnic group." This disparate group is
the largest minority in the United States, making up about 17
percent of the US population.

That number is set to grow in the twenty-first century. The
white majority is diminishing as a proportion of the population

(especially in the southern states) in a country that is already struggling to be fully integrated. Estimates of population figures vary, but most experts agree that the white majority could cease to exist in a few decades. Including Hispanics, nonwhites currently make up about 40 percent of the population. This figure is predicted to rise to 53 percent by 2050, with Hispanics composing about 29 percent, making them the fastest-growing ethnic group over the next thirty years. To those who see this trend as a real concern, building a wall and potentially stopping the influx of immigrants holds out the hope of curbing this demographic shift, although in reality it will do little to alter it.

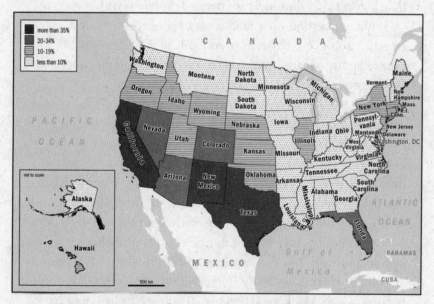

Hispanic proportion of state populations across the USA (2014).

The anti-immigration rhetoric that tends to accompany support for the wall creates further tensions among the American population. Immigrants are regularly painted in a negative light, with Trump describing them as "bad hombres": "When Mexico sends its people, they're not sending their best. . . . They're sending people that have lots of problems, and they're bringing those problems with us. They're bringing drugs. They're bringing crime. They're rapists. And some, I assume, are good people." This type of language has contributed to the rising levels of reported discrimination against Latinos over the past decade. A 2016 Pew Research poll, for example, found that 52 percent of Hispanics say they have been treated unfairly because of their ethnicity, a figure that rose to 65 percent among eighteen- to twenty-nine-year-olds. Interestingly, this was the same figure for the same age group of black people, but overall Hispanics were far less likely than blacks to say they had experienced problems with *el racismo*.

Without question, enormous advances have been made in racial equality, and every day tens of millions of Americans of all skin tones happily coexist, intermingle, eat, work, and play together. Yet racism is still a major issue across the country.

While the fast-growing Hispanic population certainly faces discrimination, the clearest racial divide in the United States is between white and black, which originated in the time of slavery and continues today. The negative effect this has on people's lives is clear: by almost all measures, being born black in America makes you more likely to be less well-off, less educated, and less healthy than being born white. This is not universally true: a well-off, middle-class, black suburban family probably has more opportunities in life than an impoverished white rural one. A Brookings Institution study suggests that whatever your ethnic group—white, black, or Hispanic—if you are from a poor background, even with a college degree your earnings in later life will be lower than those of a person from a wealthier family.

But, that said, as a rule of thumb, in the lottery of life the odds are not good if you are black. Historical and contemporary racism is clearly a major factor in the startling disparities between ethnic groups. This is true even at the very beginning of life. In the richest country on earth infant mortality is 4.8 per 1,000 births among the white population, but 11.7 for black people—roughly equivalent to that of a middle-ranking nation such as Mexico.

Lower health, lower wealth, and lower expectations all contribute to lower education levels as well, which become apparent as early as age two. By then, according to Organisation for Economic Co-operation and Development (OECD) and US education statistics, slightly fewer black children than white ones are demonstrating proficiency in development skills. By three to five years old the gap grows slightly again in reading ability; this is thought to be linked to a relative lack of reading materials in black homes, parents having less time to spend reading to children, and possibly a lack of interest in the books due to a dearth of non-white characters. As we move up through the school system, we find black Americans being suspended and/or expelled at three times the rate of white students. In schools where the majority of pupils are from minority groups, the teachers also tend to be less experienced and less well paid.

Behind these figures is daily life in what is often a low-income single-parent household. Twenty-five percent of black parents say their children are in unsafe neighborhoods, whereas for white parents the ratio is 7 percent. By the time we reach high school graduation age, we find that black Americans are twice as likely as their white counterparts to drop out. One study says that if white American and black American high school educational attainment rates were measured as if each were from a separate country, the former would be equivalent to the UK and the latter Chile. At college level, 36.2 percent of whites complete a degree, as opposed to 22.5 percent of blacks. After taking those degrees into the workplace, black Americans then earn less. Black Americans are also more likely to go to jail: they make up approximately 13 percent of the American population, but compose 38 percent of inmates.

So it goes, from the cradle to the grave. America is a violent country compared to Europe, but if you are black, it is an even more dangerous place. Murder rates for the white population are 2.5 deaths per 100,000 people. For black Americans it is 19.4, on a par with many third world or developing nations. Statistics vary, but according to CNN, if you're young, black, and male you are nearly three times more likely to be shot and killed by a police officer than your white counterpart. No wonder the life expectancy of black Americans is four years less than that of whites. Together with a number of shootings of unarmed black men in recent years, these stark figures have caused unrest and protests across the country—for example the riots in Ferguson, Missouri, in 2014—and have given rise to movements such as Black Lives Matter. With the reactions of both officials and communities under great scrutiny in the aftermath of each incident, this has become an increasingly divisive issue.

The stats highlighting the problems are easy to find. Explaining their cause is more difficult, but racism clearly still plays a part in American society. It is impossible to get away from the beginning—slavery. The slaves were emancipated, but most were left impoverished, facing societal discrimination; in these circumstances it was difficult for them to achieve parity with the dominant population quickly. How long is quickly? Well, it's been more than one hundred and fifty years, and despite the advances that have been made, especially in the last fifty, it is blindingly obvious that more needs to be done.

Race isn't the only divide in the USA. One of America's great strengths has been that the state is secular, but the country has a diversity of private religious belief and places of worship. Its faith remains overwhelmingly Christian, split between a variety of Protestant groups and Catholics, but since the 1960s other faiths have gained significant numbers of believers. About 80 percent of Americans identify themselves as Christian, Protestants being the most numerous at 46.6 percent of the population as a whole, followed by Catholics at 20.8 percent. After this come Jews (1.9 percent), Mormons (1.6 percent), Muslims (0.9 percent), Buddhists (0.7 percent), Hindu (0.7 percent), and a plethora of other smaller groups.

Does all this amount to a melting pot? Up to a point. The ideal underpinning *E pluribus unum* has survived to an extent, despite some glaring examples of inconsistency and hypocrisy. Nevertheless, in the present century the spirit of assimilation within a multiethnic society has been challenged by multiculturalism. The racial and ethnic divides play into many of the divisions in American society and have helped give rise to the politics of identity, which so plagues the republic. More and more Americans identify themselves by their ethnicity, religion, or sexuality, thereby further polarizing and splintering the nation. Different ethnicities have been encouraged to retain an overt sense of identity; instead of leading to an acceptance of diversity, this approach seems in some cases to result in some separation of certain groups from the rest of society, leaving them increasingly open to discrimination.

We saw this during the 2016 presidential election campaign when Donald Trump criticized the parents of Humayun Khan, a decorated Muslim American officer killed in Iraq, after Humayun's father spoke out against Trump's call to ban Muslim immigration. Khizr and Ghazala Khan are what Americans call "Gold Star parents." The term dates back to World War I, when families with loved ones fighting abroad flew flags with a blue star for each immediate family member. If the family member was killed, the blue star was replaced with a gold one.

Mr. Trump would hardly have used the same tone in his verbal attacks on the Khans had the family been white Christians. In American politics Gold Star parents are considered off-limits to critics because of the sacrifice the family has made for the nation. Mr. Trump said that he too had made "sacrifices" due to the number of jobs he had created in America. He suggested that Mrs. Khan had not been allowed to speak by her husband, hinting that this was because of their religion. No matter that Mr. Khan used to take the young Humayun to the Jefferson Memorial and read to him the words therein inscribed: "We hold these truths to be self-evident, that all men are created equal." Behind candidate Trump's remarks seemed to be the idea that this Gold Star family was different from others. He also seemed to be speaking to and for a section of America that defines *American* in a narrow way. Senator John McCain, a Republican and a former prisoner of war in Vietnam, voiced the opinion of much of the rest of the country when he said of Trump, "While our party has bestowed upon him the nomination, it is not accompanied by unfettered license to defame those who are the best among us."

The idea of "difference" is played upon by both the Right and the Left; this aspect of the politics of identity is exacerbating the divisions in the USA. Though united by the idea of the nation, many groups are nevertheless pulling away from one another. This can also be seen in the increasing divergence in the political arena.

Two years before the bitter Trump/Sanders/Clinton clash of 2016, the Pew Research Center conducted its largest-ever study of American political attitudes. It found that people's views were increasingly entrenched, with a growing reluctance to accept others' opinions. For example, 38 percent of politically engaged Democrats described themselves as "consistent liberals," up from 8 percent in 1994, while 33 percent of Republicans were "consistently conservative," up from 23 percent twenty years earlier. More worrying was the increased numbers of Republicans and Democrats who had contempt for one another, especially among those who were politically active. In 1994, 17 percent of Republicans had *very* unfavorable impressions of Democrats, but this has now risen to 43 percent. For the other side the figures were 16 percent rising to 38 percent.

This phenomenon has a geographical basis, with committed Democratic Party voters increasingly to be found in larger metropolitan areas, and Republicans in small towns and rural areas. Preston Stovall, an academic at the University of Nevada, Las Vegas, writes of *urban globalists* and *non-urban nationalists*, which he believes "better approximates the divide than 'Democrat' and 'Republican.'" He laments that the ideas of the non-urban are "reduced to the rantings of the ignorant," while those of the urban are "rendered as elitist and morally depraved":

> I am dismayed by the way urban Americans tend to look down on rural and agrarian communities. I do not recall a time when an offhand denigrating remark about rural Americans was ever given anything but a pass or affirmation. . . . We need to avoid the tendency to think that Republican voters are uneducated racists, and that Democrat voters are elitist reprobates.

It's important to remember that these terms and statistics mostly relate to the politically active; outside ideological silos and echo chambers there is more acceptance of the other and a greater willingness to compromise. Even so, this growing intolerance of opposing views has led to the increasingly violent rhetoric we hear in the mainstream media and the strident versions we find on the internet. The relatively placid broadcasting days of the three main TV networks' evening news programs have given way to the rise of politically competing twenty-four-hour cable news channels, shock jocks, and an ungoverned internet space where insults and death threats are the norm. The rise of twenty-four-hour social media platforms has also given a megaphone to the extremists, while the general news media has amplified that megaphone, resulting in the impression that Americans are constantly at one another's throats (or Twitter feeds), whereas most are getting along daily. Some of the younger generation are now the most intolerant, many of whom are pushing back against the ideals of free speech and arguing that political intolerance is justified against people with whom they disagree.

Extremism is also conducted in America's educational establishments by a small minority of students with some support from professors. Large numbers of the older generation of academics increasingly resemble deer caught in the headlights as their revolutionary children turn against the very people who taught them to be so ideological. In a nasty intellectual atmosphere in America, intimidating, baiting "no platformers" push forward with timid, intellectually weak professors in retreat. This endangers cohesiveness because the shrillness of these campaigns is amplified in online discourse. If increasing numbers of students leave college having been radicalized, whether to the left or the right, their extreme views may become more prevalent.

One of the best examples of this came in 2017 at Evergreen State College in Washington. A liberal-minded white professor, Bret Weinstein, objected to the idea that the college had to explain and justify any teaching appointments on the grounds of race. He then disagreed with a student body request that on a specific day white students should not attend classes in order to create a safe environment for students of color to debate issues. His classroom was subsequently invaded by students screaming about racism and white privilege. They demanded that he and two other staff be fired, and when the college president, George Bridges, tried to mediate, he was repeatedly sworn at and told to be quiet. A video of the original incident shows students shrieking questions at Weinstein; when he asks them, "Would you like to hear the answer or not?," they shout, "No!" The incident was emblematic of the increasingly frenzied attempts to shame people with different views, where one group convinces itself that another is the epitome of evil and shouldn't be given the opportunity to express its ideas. It may be childish, it may be simplistic, but it is also dangerous and threatens the ideal of free speech.

This modern closure of the American mind comes from both sides of the political spectrum and is reducing the space in the middle. Among the worst perpetrators are those actively seeking to promote suspicion and hatred of the other side. At one extreme they include both white and black separatist groups, some of whom are armed; demonstrations often result in violence. In 2017, for example, Charlottesville, Virginia, was the scene of a protest against the removal of a statue of the Confederate commander Robert E. Lee; but white supremacist groups also paraded with Nazi flags, voicing racist and anti-Semitic slogans. Violence ensued, resulting in the death of counterdemonstrator Heather Heyer, who was run over and killed by a white supremacist. The ensuing outrage was exacerbated by Trump's response: he repeatedly refused to condemn the alt-right, including the KKK and neo-Nazis, stating that both sides had been violent.

Across the divide, and yet not so far away, are the black separatist groups; they may well be a reaction to white society's discrimination, but nevertheless their ideology is racist. A classic example is the Nation of Islam, whose leader, Louis Farrakhan, believes that sixty-six hundred years ago a black scientist called Yakub created the white people as "blue-eyed devils" designed to be inherently evil and ungodly. Mr. Farrakhan has also said that Jews practice a "gutter religion" and prey on black people; his solution to the problems faced by blacks is to support racial separatism and end interracial relationships.

Among the most famous of all great American speeches is Abraham Lincoln's "House Divided." He gave it in 1858 when accepting the Illinois Republican Party's nomination for senator. The phrase comes from the Bible in the Gospel of Mark 3:25, Luke 11:17, and Matthew 12:25. Jesus says, "And if a house be divided against itself, that house cannot stand." Lincoln was referring to the split over slavery, but now the USA finds itself deeply divided once more: rifts over race, ethnicity, and political leanings are all causing tensions and emotions to flare up.

America's increasingly divided house needs a more rational, conciliatory, and open-minded approach, but the debate is too often conducted—by both Right and Left—with hysteria and a fanatical determination to use identity politics to drown out "the other." In this febrile atmosphere, Trump's rhetoric about the wall plays on historical and new divisions within the nation, speaking of a narrow definition of *American*. The racial, ethnic, and political divides all coalesce in this question of the wall—of what the USA is, what it should be, and how it carries forward its ideals of freedom and equality.

Barack Obama was hardly the most successful of America's presidents and, like all the others, had policies that were divisive, but underpinning his view of his country was a conviction that a nation is stronger, and a better place, when it embraces the idea of *E pluribus unum*. He is already fading into history, but his place there is assured and is an example of what can be achieved by modern America. It is exemplified by his speech to the Democratic National Convention in 2004:

> The pundits like to slice and dice our country into . . . red states for Republicans, blue states for Democrats. . . . But I've got news for them. . . . We worship an awesome God in the blue states, and we don't like federal agents poking around in our libraries in the red states. We coach Little League in the blue states, and, yes, we've got gay friends in the red states. . . . We are one people.

CHAPTER 3

Israel and Palestine

You see the trouble we are in, how Jerusalem lies in ruins with its gates burned. Come, let us build the wall of Jerusalem, that we may no longer suffer derision.

—Book of Nehemiah 2:17

Previous pages: Palestinian men waiting to cross the wall through a checkpoint outside Bethlehem, in the West Bank.

Within minutes of driving south from the Old City walls in Jerusalem, the new walls of Bethlehem rise up in the distance. As you approach, you see twenty-six-foot-high slabs of concrete, topped with barbed wire. Some sections are electrified, and interspersed are high watchtowers with dusty thick bulletproof glass, from behind which young Israeli soldiers look down on both zones. In the Israeli sector there is open ground, but once you are through a checkpoint and on the other side, you can drive along streets just wide enough for a car, with low apartment buildings facing the wall opposite. It is dispiriting, intimidating, oppressive, and otherworldly. Homes and high walls are not supposed to be this close to each other.

Crossing the border is thoroughly depressing, but doubly so when you do so at the parts made of concrete, as most outsiders do. These are the sections placed next to urban areas to prevent sniper fire from taller buildings. Much of the rest of the 440-mile-long barrier is a fence.

Despite the fact that only 3 percent of the "separation barrier" between Israel and the Palestinian West Bank is made of concrete, it is routinely referred to as "the wall." Why? Because the 3 percent is far more visually arresting than the other 97 percent. What TV crew or photographer would use a barbed-wire fence as a background when a twenty-six-foot-high concrete barrier overseen by watchtowers and covered in graffiti can be the focus? This is understandable for human interest, and because of the impact of the starkness of a wall, and what it says about a conflict and a divide. Whatever the barrier is called, it remains a monument to one of the world's most intractable disputes.

At the concrete sections, the British propaganda artist Banksy has made use of the strange juxtaposition of the wall and daily life. For several years he has been painting murals on the Palestinian side. Some are now famous: a little girl frisks an Israel Defense Forces (IDF) soldier for weapons; a white dove wears a bullet-proof vest; a girl is carried over a wall by balloons. In a possibly apocryphal story, a Palestinian man is said to have once told the artist that he had made the wall look beautiful. Banksy thanked the man, only to be told, "We don't want it to be beautiful. We hate this wall. Go home."

A less "beautiful" image often found on sections of the wall is that of Handala, a forlorn barefoot ten-year-old refugee boy. Handala, originally drawn by the late Palestinian artist Naji al-Ali, usually has his back to us—suggesting he will not turn around until there is justice for the Palestinians. Al-Ali, who also criticized Arab leaders, himself left and never returned to Palestine. He was shot in the face in London in July 1987 and died five weeks later. A Palestinian man the British police said was a member of the Palestine Liberation Organization (PLO) was arrested in connection with the assassination, but never charged.

Recalling al-Ali and Handala, I was reminded of a Palestinian friend back in London. He is from Bethlehem but left in the late 1980s and says he would not "turn around," meaning return. "I cannot face going through the Israeli checkpoints to get to my own home," he told me. "It would be like an admission of their authority."

Banksy returned, though, and went several steps further. To mark the hundredth anniversary of the 1917 Balfour Declaration, which promised Jews a homeland in what was then called Pales-tine, he opened the Walled Off Hotel in the West Bank. All ten bedrooms face the wall, which is four yards across the street. It has, said Banksy, "the worst view of any hotel in the world," but it "offers a warm welcome to people from all sides of the conflict and across the world." Many visitors to Bethlehem now want to see the view, creating what critics describe as "conflict tourism"; but supporters say it plays a part in building bridges between Palestine and the outside world. Nevertheless, Banksy tours, Banksy memorabilia, and selfies with Banksy art are now de rigueur for many tourists visiting the birthplace of Jesus.

At the hotel a narrow terrace houses chairs and tables where drinks are served to tourists who have ventured away from the usual historical Christian sites. From the terrace you can read graffiti on the wall, from the whimsical MAKE HUMMUS NOT WALLS to the hopeful GOD WILL DESTROY THIS WALL to swastikas formed from the shape of the Star of David. The hotel's interior is decorated with icons of the Palestinian resistance to Israeli rule, such as slingshots and damaged security cameras. The bedrooms feature Banksy murals, including one of an Israeli soldier and a Palestinian protester having a pillow fight. Downstairs, a small museum outlines the history of the conflict, and at its entrance is a life-size model of the British diplomat Arthur Balfour. At the click of a button his mechanized right arm begins to move as he signs his famous declaration.

What is missing from the artwork is anything depicting the Israeli rationale for the stark ugliness facing the hotel. The narrow street has no room for an artistic depiction of a bombed-out Israeli bus; then again, art is not required to be neutral. But on the wall, one piece of graffiti, perhaps unintentionally, hints at one aspect of the other side's view: THIS WALL MAY TAKE CARE OF THE PRESENT, BUT IT HAS NO FUTURE. In politics, the present is often more important than the future, especially when you want to be elected.

Why the wall exists and what it achieves are disputed. The border between the two countries has seen violent controversy ever since Israel came into being, starting with the Arab-Israeli War in 1948. At the end of that conflict a cease-fire line was agreed to, the Green Line. But in 1967, during the Six-Day War, Israel occupied the West Bank and Gaza, as well as the Sinai region and the Golan Heights. After two decades of living under Israeli rule, Palestinian frustration and anger spread across the Palestinian territories, leading to violent uprisings and protests in the First Intifada (1987–93). *Intifada* derives from the Arabic word *nafada*, meaning "shake off," and in this sense translates as freedom from oppression. After some years of fragile peace, during which Israel continued to occupy Gaza, the decades-long land dispute exploded in sustained violence again in 2000, and at the outbreak of this Second Intifada the wall started to go up.

The Palestinian view is that the barrier is an excuse for a land grab and to put "facts on the ground," carving out the contours of a possible two-state solution but on Israeli terms, which would result in Palestine losing at least 10 percent of the West Bank land, as the wall's current position lies well inside Palestinian territory. Israel cites topographical reasons for the path of the wall, but in certain areas it strays east of the Green Line, around Jewish settlements.

About four hundred thousand Jews live in the West Bank. The term *settlements* suggests small encampments, perhaps located on arid, windswept hills. However, although many started that way, some have grown into full-scale towns complete with town halls, supermarkets, and schools. The roads that connect them to each other, and to Israel, make it difficult for Palestinians to move about in the West Bank or to maintain large regions of contiguous territory. More than two hundred thousand Jews now also live in East Jerusalem, which Israel annexed in 1967 but which the Palestinians claim as the capital of a future Palestinian state. Israeli Jews tend to think of East Jerusalem and the West Bank as separate entities; no such division exists in Palestinian minds.

The separation barrier roughly follows the route of the
Green Line, established in the 1949 Armistice Agreements,
but in several places extends into the Palestinian side.

The issue of the settlements divides Israeli public opinion; the wisdom, legality, and morality of their existence are always fiercely debated. The religious Jewish settlers claim they can live in the West Bank because it was part of ancient Israel and was promised to them in the Bible. Secular settlers argue that Israel took the territory from Jordan, which subsequently dropped its claim to the land, and that therefore their presence is not illegal—a view not shared by the international community.

"Look at those walls!" says a Palestinian friend, involved in civic society, who prefers not to be named. "They are disgusting! It's all part of a plan to steal land. They move the wall hundreds of yards into Palestinian land so that later they can say we must negotiate for it even though it was ours all along." As we drive alongside the wall, he gestures angrily toward Palestinian areas, which were once planted with olive trees, now uprooted to create a no-man's-land, which he fears will one day be Israeli territory. "They have always done this. Create what they call facts on the ground, but it's their facts, and it's our ground."

The Israelis have a very different view of the wall; even the graffiti and artwork on their side of the barrier tells a different story. Some is anti-Palestinian and makes the case for the necessity of the wall; some is pro-Palestinian and depicts their suffering; but a lot consists simply of images of landscapes designed to make the wall "invisible"—and that is what it is to the majority of the Israeli population. Most of those inside Israel have little reason to go near it, or through it. Most don't go to the Jewish settlements inside the West Bank, and for the settlers who do travel back and forth, it's just part of a distant terrain through which they get priority passage.

The majority of Israelis are in favor of the wall and believe that it has had a positive effect. The Israeli government points out that in the three years before it went up, a spate of suicide bombings and attacks by Palestinians had killed hundreds of Israelis. The bomb makers and bombers once operated freely out of towns in the West Bank that were less than an hour's drive from such targets as Tel Aviv, Netanya, and Jerusalem. In the three years following the completion of the first phase of the wall, just over sixty Israelis were killed. This is the Israeli justification for the wall—it is simply a security measure designed to stop the killings. A minority of Israelis oppose it; they see the barrier—and particularly the existing route it takes—as an obstacle to agreeing on a lasting, peaceful solution with the Palestinians. Most of them are on the left of Israeli politics, and they can be vocal in their protests, but even within the Left they are a minority. With the murders of civilians at a relatively low level, many Israelis have psychologically retreated behind the barrier. They have many other problems, and divisions, with which to deal, and safe-behind-the-wall economics now sometimes trumps security in surveys of national concerns.

David Kornbluth, one of Israel's most distinguished diplomats, now retired, believes in a two-state solution and says he "feel[s] for the plight of the Palestinians," but on the security barrier he has a clear-eyed, stark, direct, and uncompromising view, echoed by many: "The wall is a huge success. It stopped the suicide bombers from killing. There wouldn't be a security barrier at all if it hadn't been necessary. It's a huge cost; nobody wanted it, not the left, not the party in government. In my opinion the unfortunate, unwanted disturbances to the Palestinians do not balance against the prevention of the loss of life the barrier has brought. Of course I feel for their plight, but that has nothing to do with them trying to kill hundreds of our civilians." I remind him that those who are against the barrier regard it as a symbol of oppression and the power of the oppressor. "It's nothing to do with being a symbol of power or oppression; if it was, we'd have put it up in 1967. It's there to answer a practical need."

In a way, it's putting into practice the ideology of Ze'ev (Vladimir) Jabotinsky (1880–1940) and his theory of the "iron wall." Jabotinsky was an ideologue in the pre-independence Jewish community in Palestine. He was the principal architect of the strategy for dealing with the Arabs, who vehemently opposed the formation of Israel, from a position of unassailable military strength. Only once the Arab side had realized it could not destroy Israel, he argued, would it come to the table and make deals. "It is my hope and belief," Jabotinsky declared, "that we will then offer them guarantees that will satisfy them and that both peoples will live in peace as good neighbours. But the sole way to such an agreement is through the iron wall."

As the barrier has gradually enclosed the West Bank, suicide bombings and gun attacks in Israel have fallen dramatically, and the Israeli government says the barrier and the statistics are directly correlated. Critics, however, disagree. They argue that it was constructed at the same time as Israel's enemies deliberately lowered the tempo of attacks, having decided that the suicide bombings were harming their cause in the eyes of the outside world, and that they weren't worth the high cost of the Israeli responses. Fawaz Gerges, professor of international relations at the London School of Economics, believes this to be the case: "Hamas and other Palestinian factions have made a conscious decision to desist from carrying out attacks inside Israel because of political and strategic liabilities."

Nevertheless, Israel maintains that the wall plays a crucial role in the country's security, along with the other barriers it has constructed to maintain control over its borders. In addition to the one in the West Bank, Israel built a security barrier on the border with Gaza; begun in 1994, it's nearly 40 miles long. Also, a 152-mile-long fence along the Egyptian-Israeli border was completed in 2013 and has halted illegal immigration from a variety of African countries. Between 2000 and 2012 almost fifty thousand

Africans, mostly from Sudan, Eritrea, and Ethiopia, crossed that border after frequently harrowing journeys, often being shot at by Egyptian border patrols. Most have settled in Israel because of legal barriers to their deportation, and the reluctance of African countries to take them back. A fourth fence, less publicized, was built along the Syrian border after that country plunged into civil war. With various jihadist groups, such as the Nusra Front and Islamic State (IS), advancing close to the border on the Syrian side of the Golan Heights, Israel again began shoring up its defenses.

So, if Israel is certain that these walls are responsible for the decrease in violence, are they now a permanent fixture? This is a divisive issue, but many people don't see them as a lasting solution to the problems in the region, merely as a step toward it, and say the walls should just be temporary. Mr. Kornbluth, one of the diplomats involved in drawing the outlines of the barrier, says, "The final settlement comes in stages. . . . I think the wall will go, and it's not necessarily on the line of any eventual boundary, that's not what it's for, it's to significantly lower terror. . . . It can come down as quickly as it went up. I'm extremely clear about that." For that to happen an agreement will be needed not only between the two sides, but also within them—and they are both deeply divided.

Israel encapsulates the concept of division in many ways, with very different people living side by side—or, in some cases, unable to live side by side.

Israel is a new nation, and a melting pot. This small country has a population of 8.6 million, but those people come from many different ethnic backgrounds. More than a million Russians, for example, arrived in Israel in the 1990s when its population was only 5 million. Reflecting the many rifts in Israeli society, its politics is divided—more so than in most democracies—with left-wing political parties, right-wing parties, Arab parties, and religious parties, and further subdivisions within those categories.

The first Israeli census came in 1948, the year the State of Israel was declared. Then, 86 percent of the population was Jewish, 9 percent Muslim, 3 percent Christian, and 1 percent Druze. In the 2014 census, the Muslim population had almost doubled to 16.9 percent, the Druze to 2 percent, while the Jewish proportion had declined to 75 percent and the Christian to 2 percent. The remaining 4 percent is made up of a variety of minorities.

However, even the Jewish majority is deeply divided. Most fall into one of two categories—either Ashkenazi or Sephardi. All ultimately trace their roots back to Israel before the scattering of the tribes by the Romans, but the Ashkenazi are often lighter skinned, and their more recent origin is European. The Sephardi are named after the Hebrew word for Spain—*Sepharad*—and are mostly made up of the hundreds of thousands of Jews forced out of Arab countries following the declaration of the State of Israel in 1948.

The Ashkenazi have tended to be the elite and have largely dominated politics and business since the state's inception, partly because so many of them were well educated, and partly because they had arrived in Israel in the late nineteenth and early twentieth centuries, decades before the Sephardi fled the Arab pogroms. In recent years, though, the Sephardi have grown in influence, and their religious parties often hold the balance of power and are therefore invited into coalition governments. There are few practical religious differences between the two sects, but the cultural and political dissimilarities influenced by their Middle Eastern and European backgrounds mean that while intermarriage is not rare, it is still not the norm. In culture, in both music and food choices, the Sephardi are far more Middle Eastern than the Ashkenazi, whose diet is rooted in that of Eastern European Jewry.

Whether Ashkenazi or Sephardi, the Jewish population has

another, more stringent religious divide: between the secular (49 percent), traditional (29 percent), religious (13 percent), and ultra-Orthodox (9 percent), also known as the Haredim, the "ones who tremble in awe of God." Across these categories, the majority would list their religion as Jewish: 87 percent of the secular still attend a Passover service, and half say they light candles on Friday nights. But the many clear differences between the groups are visible throughout society.

All these groups live together in one small country and speak the same language, but they rarely interact socially. Many neighborhoods are divided along these lines, and whole swathes of Jerusalem, and parts of Tel Aviv and other cities, are almost exclusively secular or religious. Intermarriage between the two is unusual. Many secular Jews say they would be as uncomfortable with one of their children marrying a Haredi as with a Christian. These children will probably have been educated at segregated institutions—the Haredim at gender-separated Haredi schools, the secular at nonreligious schools.

Urban areas have mixed religious/secular neighborhoods, but even here you can tell in seconds who is Orthodox and who is not. Even the type of yarmulke the religious men wear on their heads can say something about their beliefs. For example, as a badge of recognition many West Bank settlers wear knitted yarmulkes, which are larger than the felt ones worn by the modern Orthodox and some Haredim. Cognoscenti of these matters can tell which rabbi a Haredi man follows from the type of fur hat he is wearing. The ultrareligious and secular, on the other hand, are almost invisible to each other. This is a two-way street. The Haredi man with a fur hat, sidelocks, and white stockings, wearing what looks to outsiders like a dressing gown, is not about to ask a secular woman for directions, and vice versa.

The economic difference between the groups is clear as well. Israel's economy does relatively well compared to those of most countries, but its prosperity is unevenly distributed, and the gaps between different groups are widening. Poverty is widespread—one in five Israelis live in households whose income is less than half the national average (double the average for the OECD countries)—and the Haredim tend to be worse off, for a number of reasons. Large families contribute to poverty, and the Haredim tend to have more children than the modern Orthodox and the secular. In Pew Research polling, 28 percent of the Haredim said they had seven children or more, whereas only 1 percent of the secular had this many. The Haredim are also more likely to be unemployed, as large numbers choose to study the Torah rather than work.

You can see these rifts within Jewish society wherever you go, although they are particularly prominent at religious sites. Take, for example, the Western Wall, the supporting wall of the remains of the Second Temple, which was destroyed by the Romans in 70 CE. Religious scholars have mixed opinions about how holy it is because it was not part of the inner sanctum. Nevertheless, it is a place of great importance to almost all Jews, religious or not. Above it is the Al-Aqsa compound, which houses the Dome of the Rock, built in the seventh century and considered to be Islam's third most holy site. Israeli and Palestinian Muslims, and foreign tourists, are allowed to visit the compound, which the Arabs call the Noble Sanctuary, but Jews are mostly forbidden entry, a policy the government usually upholds on security grounds.

Approaching the Western Wall you immediately see the divide. A fence running from the plaza to the wall separates the open space into a one-third/two-thirds split. On the smaller, right-hand side you see women, on the left-hand side the men. A few religious movements in Israel have mixed congregations in their synagogues, but they are a tiny minority and have almost no influence on religious matters. The Orthodox synagogues are more powerful, and their congregations are separated by gender; so, therefore, is the Western Wall.

Not all women are happy with the situation; some believe they should be able to pray as a group and wear prayer shawls, as do men. This has led to a bitter dispute between a group called Women of the Wall (WOW), who have held services at the site, and the Haredim, who have sought—often violently—to prevent them. The debate has raged for thirty years, ever since the first one hundred or so women prayed at the wall and were disrupted by both verbal and physical assaults from Haredi men and women. That set the pattern for a dispute that is still being fought in the courts and at the Western Wall plaza.

When WOW appears for their monthly prayer meeting, they are often pushed and spat at by both men and women and always require police protection. In 2013 buses featuring posters in support of the women had their windows smashed as they drove through ultra-Orthodox neighborhoods in Jerusalem. The Talmud explicitly states that God destroyed the Second Temple because of the hatred of one Jew toward another—an irony that may have been lost on some of the participants.

These differences within society also affect the political sphere. Most in the secular category see themselves as Israeli first and Jewish second; most Orthodox see themselves as Jewish first and then Israeli; and this influences and informs political divisions. Sephardi Israelis tend to lean to the right in politics, while the Ashkenazi are more split. The more religious sects tend to support mainly religious political parties, while the Haredim will simply vote as their rabbi tells them to. Religious political parties are thus almost always components in coalition governments, and they often hold diametrically opposed views on many key topics, including religious conversion, conscription, the West Bank settlements, marriage, divorce, and gender segregation.

The religious parties tend to dominate matters of education and religion, and their views are not necessarily in line with those of the rest of the population. The ultra-Orthodox campaign ceaselessly to keep the right to oversee marriage ceremonies within their jurisdiction and try to enforce, often violently, their view that no one should drive on the Sabbath, especially not in their neighborhoods—sometimes reinforcing that belief with roadblocks to prevent cars from passing through. Many oppose any form of compromise on territory with the Palestinians: while 66 percent of Jewish Israelis overall support a two-state solution to the conflict, around 60 percent of those who vote for a religious party favor a one-state outcome.

Secular Israelis, meanwhile, bitterly resent that, despite ongoing political and legal battles, the ultra-Orthodox do not have to serve in the military, yet at the same time receive government funding to support their communities and projects. The secular also fear being outnumbered and driven out of Jerusalem, as the birth rate among the religious sects is so much higher—which is also seen as an economic threat to the country, as such a high proportion of the Haredim are unemployed.

David Kornbluth says that all the "racial" religious and class divisions and sometimes contrary positions among Israeli Jews mask an underlying unity in the face of outside threats, when the population tends to fall into line: "Israel is an extremely strong cohesive country at time of war. . . . When war comes the country is united. A lot of people say the real threat to Israel is the divisions, that they are what could bring it down. But it remains a seriously strong country." Strong maybe; but however united the Jewish Israelis might be, another divide—between them and Israel's Arab population—will probably never be bridged without equality inside Israel and an equitable two-state solution with the Palestinians.

Most of Israel's Arabs, a fifth of the population, do not want to live in an impoverished Palestine and know that, as Israelis, their living standards are higher than those of most other Arabs in the Middle East. But that does not mean they are satisfied with their lot—quite the opposite. While Israel's Arabs have dramatically increased in number, and their birth rate is higher than that of their Jewish neighbors, they have not kept pace in economic and social terms. As their numbers grow, so might their political clout, as they will be able to elect more Arab politicians to the Knesset (parliament); but in the medium term their limited voting power is unlikely to change the political makeup of Israeli governments.

Israeli Arabs have full citizenship, with social and religious rights guaranteed under law. They run their own political parties, newspapers, and broadcast outlets. Arabs sit on the Supreme Court; they play for the national soccer team. Nevertheless, despite living in the same country as Israelis, and having equality in law, in many ways they live separate lives.

Most Israeli Arab children are educated in Arabic-speaking schools. They live in Arab villages, or, if in urban areas, in Arab districts. Haifa is probably Israel's most mixed city, but even there you see clear delineations between neighborhoods. When Arab children grow up, they will read Arab newspapers and listen to Arab broadcasts, and even when they watch national TV shows, they will find themselves underrepresented. Almost all will speak fluent Hebrew, but only use it in shared workplaces. Like the Haredim, they are more usually at the bottom of the earnings pyramid, but while many of the ultra-Orthodox choose not to work, the Israeli Arabs often lack access to higher-paid jobs. Poverty rates are at 50 percent for Arab families, with similarly high levels for Haredim.

For decades public spending on education per child was significantly lower in Arab localities, although a five-year plan introduced in 2016 is supposed to be addressing this. Eight of Israel's ten poorest towns are Arab, with lower educational standards contributing to this poverty. Around 79 percent of Israeli Arabs believe they are discriminated against. Successive governments have tried to legislate against this and have set job quotas for minority groups in the public sector, but they are rarely met, and the laws lack teeth.

The non-Jewish communities are also split along various religious and ethnic lines—between, for example, settled Muslims,
bedouin, Christians, and the Druze. Some fare worse than others
within the Arab populations; the Christians, for example, tend to
find themselves more on the socioeconomic level of Jewish Israelis,
while the bedouin are the most disadvantaged of all the indigenous
groups in Israel. They try to live apart from everyone else but are
finding it increasingly hard to so do in the twenty-first century.
Land disputes between the state and bedouin tribes have ensured
that almost half the two-hundred-thousand-strong population now
live in "unrecognized villages," some without water or electricity.
Their days of nomadic living are almost at an end, and even the
few who do still try to move their livestock certainly can't roam
the entire region as they did before the coming of the nation-state.

The bedouin experience is slightly different from that of the
rest of the Arab community. For one thing, they have less emotional attachment to "nationhood," which is one of the reasons
why some volunteer each year to serve in the IDF, despite being
exempt from military service, as are their fellow Muslim Israelis.
A few non-bedouin Israeli Muslims do volunteer for military service, along with some Israeli Christian Arabs, and many Druze,
but for the majority of non-Jewish Israelis this is a no-go. Many,
probably most, Israeli Arabs self-identify as Palestinian. Because
service in the IDF often means operating in the West Bank and
at the border crossings, this would be viewed as participating in
the oppression of fellow Arabs or fellow Palestinians. The Israeli
state would not agree that any form of oppression is taking place,
but is wise enough to know that compulsory military service for
Arab citizens simply wouldn't work.

This "Arabness" is the one thing that unites Arabs on both sides
of the border—it's an identity that crosses national boundaries—but
nevertheless, many differences exist between them. We often use
oversimplified, broad-brush descriptions such as *Israelis*, *Arabs*, and

Palestinians. This can be useful shorthand for understanding politics and geopolitics at the macro level, but scratch beneath the surface and you find complexity and see the microdivisions that constitute what we perceive as the big picture, whether *Israeli* or *Palestinian*.

Once we cross into the Palestinian territories, the biggest divide is territorial. Among the many barriers to the formation of a single Palestinian state is that the West Bank and Gaza are two territories, not one. The distance between them is not the issue. If all sides could agree, the twenty-five miles of intervening Israeli territory could be overcome with a highway bridge or tunnel. However, the two regions remain separated not just by geography, but also by politics and ideology.

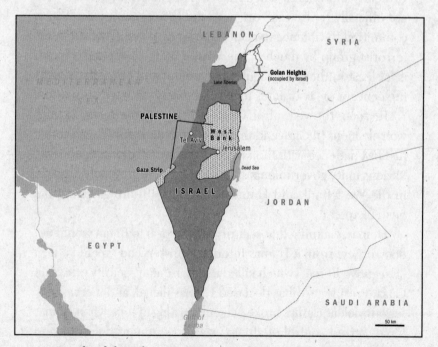

Israel and the Palestinian territories of Gaza and the West Bank.

Even if, theoretically, Israel was ready to negotiate, it could not do so because Palestinians are far from united on the topic. The relatively secular Fatah movement is the dominant political force in the Palestinian Authority, which governs the 2.5 million Palestinians in the West Bank, and the radical Islamist movement Hamas is in charge of the 1.7 million in the Gaza Strip; the two have very different ideas about what the policy toward Israel should be. Hamas remains an Islamist movement that, despite accepting in its New Charter of 2017 the possibility of a Palestinian state built on the 1967 borders, still declares in Article 20 of that document, "Hamas rejects any alternative to the full and complete liberation of Palestine, from the river to the sea," referring to the River Jordan and the Mediterranean, between which lies Israel. The New Charter waters down some of the virulently anti-Semitic language of the original charter, but it does not officially replace the original, and the organization remains committed to violence to achieve its aims. It is still considered a terrorist group by much of the West. Fatah, on the other hand, is, at least in theory, a secular movement and officially accepts the concept of "two states for two peoples."

In 2006, the year after Israel withdrew from Gaza, Hamas won elections in Gaza and the West Bank, mostly because voters had lost patience with the rampant corruption of Fatah officials. Various unity governments staggered along, with Fatah stronger in the West Bank and Hamas in Gaza, until things came to a head in 2007.

Hamas, claiming that security forces loyal to Fatah would not obey orders from a Hamas interior minister, had created a new "Executive Force," which killed a senior Fatah security official in Gaza. President Abbas declared Hamas illegal, and increasingly serious violent clashes broke out, culminating in June when Hamas forces seized control of all of Gaza's government buildings and murdered many Fatah supporters. The factional fighting killed hundreds of Palestinians before Fatah security forces fled toward the Israeli border. President Abbas denounced the events as a "coup" and cracked down on Hamas centers of power in the West Bank. Despite repeated efforts, the two sides have been unable to bridge the divide between them. Neither is prepared to cede authority, but neither enjoys full support either. In October 2017 they signed a reconciliation deal, which President Abbas hailed as a "declaration of the end to division." However, this soon ran into difficulties with both sides still claiming legitimacy. Nevertheless, a degree of unity is required for any new Middle East peace deal to even get off the ground.

Hamas, whose full name translates as "Islamic resistance movement," has enforced its version of Islam in Gaza and is trying to dominate all aspects of life. This has alienated not just the remaining Fatah supporters, but also some of the more moderate population. The small Christian community, numbering perhaps fewer than three thousand people, feels under pressure, and many are trying to leave, like so many embattled Christians across the Middle East. Hamas has continued to fire rockets indiscriminately into Israeli civilian areas or has failed to prevent other groups from so doing. This has also split opinion between those who support what they see as resistance against "the Israeli blockade," and those who believe that the retaliation this draws from Israel is not worth the largely futile acts of defiance.

Despite the Israeli withdrawal, the Gazans remain trapped between the forty-mile-long barrier built by Israel and a fence on the Egyptian border. To the west, the Gazans can look out across the Mediterranean, but in the distance they usually see an Israeli patrol boat or warship. There is no safe route out that way either. Both Israel and Egypt restrict movement in and out of the Strip, which causes great hardship, but both states argue that they believe Hamas and others would project intolerable levels of violence out of Gaza if there were free passage. Egypt is

as concerned about this as Israel because Hamas originally grew
out of the Muslim Brotherhood (MB) movement in Egypt. The
military-dominated government in Cairo, having overthrown the
short-lived MB government in 2013, does not wish to see Hamas
operating in its territory.

Israel allows hundreds of truckloads of food, medical, and
energy supplies into Gaza each day, but these imports are restricted
when cross-border hostilities break out. Hundreds of smuggling
tunnels, built under the border with Egypt, ensure a thriving black
market in all sorts of goods and a passage out for those who brave
the risk of a tunnel collapsing. I have even seen a tractor pulling a
brand-new Mercedes through, and the car showrooms in Gaza are
full, but this is hardly a basis for a normal economy. The Egyptians
have reinforced their fences over the years and sometimes flood
the tunnels to prevent arms and fighters from being smuggled into
the Sinai, which suffers from frequent terror attacks. Egyptian
and Israeli action against the tunnels does reduce the potential
for violent incursions, but at a cost to the black-market economy,
without which the trapped population suffers intensified hardships.
In 2016 Israel announced a plan to build an underground wall,
more than a hundred feet deep, to prevent armed groups from
emerging from tunnels to attack Israeli border towns.

The spring of 2018 saw weeks of violence as on consecutive
Fridays thousands of Palestinians attempted to storm the Gaza
fence with Israel to demonstrate their "right of return" to where
some of their families lived in 1948 in what is now Israel.

Dozens of Palestinians were shot dead and hundreds were
injured as Israeli soldiers used live ammunition from across the
border. Several Hamas leaders attended the demonstrations and
called on protestors to be ready to die a martyr's death. Some of
the dead and injured were Hamas fighters, some were armed, and
there were cases where the fence was breached, but most of
the casualties were unarmed and shot from a distance, prompting

allegations of a massively disproportionate use of force. Critics said the Israeli forces sometimes opened fire even when two crucial conditions of international law for using lethal force were absent: the targeted individual posed a danger and the danger was immediate.

Each side saw the events through their own prism. The Palestinians argued that the very existence of the fence demonstrated the historical injustice perpetrated against them. The Israelis said there are Israeli villages within a mile of the fence that had to be protected and that without the fence the people there would be murdered.

Across in the West Bank life is hard, but easier than in Gaza. Palestinians here can cross into Israel or Jordan, albeit sometimes with difficulty, and make their way onward. Each year tens of thousands are treated in Israeli hospitals because the health care in the West Bank is of a lower standard. Work permits are far harder to obtain. In the late 1980s Palestinians from the West Bank and Gaza made up about 8 percent of the Israeli workforce; now the figure is about 2 percent. This decline in numbers is partly because of security issues during the First and Second Intifadas, and partly because workers from other countries, mostly Asians, have taken their place.

So, behind the great security barrier live 2.5 million Palestinians asking how this state of affairs came about. In previous decades there was little debate: it was because of the partition of Palestine, supported by the outside world; then the Nakba, or "catastrophe," of losing the war to prevent the State of Israel from coming into existence in 1948; followed by the disaster of 1967 and the occupation. These factors remain the root-cause explanation for Palestinians, but they are no longer enough.

Many younger Palestinians are asking, without any softening of feeling toward Israel, why their own leadership has failed them for generations. It is generally accepted that much of the PA is corrupt, and the generation of politicians who rose to power during the Arafat and then Abbas years now have little support. Some people have turned to Hamas, still believing that force will one day turn the tide, and the divisions between Fatah and Hamas threaten a serious recurrence of the fighting of 2007—but this time in the West Bank. More are heartily sick of both major factions, and in the West Bank it is not unusual to hear it spoken, quietly, that the PA's cooperation with Israel on security makes it a "subcontractor" of the occupation.

But what to do; where, politically, to go? Palestine is hardly an open society. Dissent can lead to arrest and torture, as many Palestinian journalists can verify. Liberal democracy, as understood in the West, does not exist in Palestine. A moderate liberal party, espousing gay rights, for example, would get little traction, and propagating such views publicly would be dangerous. The few rainbow flags painted on the wall/separation barrier are always quickly covered up.

This is not surprising: the Middle East tends to be an extremely conservative region compared to Europe and North America; but the chances of a liberal democracy emerging in Palestine are also hamstrung by the Israeli occupation. Conservatives can, and do, say that the struggle for national self-determination must take priority over everything else. For these reasons the widespread dislike for the current West Bank leadership will not necessarily translate into a push for genuine liberal democracy, and the tensions between the West Bank and Gaza ensure that Palestine will remain a house divided.

The Palestinians can expect little help from their Arab neighbors. Governments in the Middle East have only ever used the Palestinians as political tools, while discriminating against the refugees they host and ensuring that they remain in squalid camps. In most Arab countries they, and their children, even if born in the country, cannot become citizens, vote, or run for office in national elections. Jordan has been more flexible than most, but even there those of Palestinian descent face discrimination and are underrepresented in parliament. In Lebanon, where more than four hundred thousand or so Palestinians live, about fifty categories of jobs remain forbidden to them; for example, they cannot become lawyers, journalists, or doctors. In both Lebanon and Syria, they are not allowed to own property and must live in the camps. Those who have circumvented the laws cannot pass on property to their children.

The rationale behind some of the discrimination is that all Palestinians, even those who are the great-grandchildren of refugees who fled in 1948, have the right of return. This does not negate the obligation to grant them human rights, but it has been convenient for the Arab governments to keep the Palestinians in poverty so that they cannot enter the mainstream of the body politic, and in order to highlight their plight so as to deflect criticism from their own failed domestic policies.

With so much division within the populations, as well as between them, establishing a two-state solution that is acceptable to all parties seems unlikely in the near future, even though many people support the concept. With so many challenges and stumbling blocks—where the border would lie, how both settlers and refugees would be dealt with, what would happen to Jerusalem—neither country seems able to put together a coherent policy that everyone endorses within its own borders, never mind one that both sides can agree on. So for the moment the barriers remain, in an attempt to contain the violence that has erupted so fiercely and frequently since Israel came into being.

The modern State of Israel was born in violence and feels it has been forced to fight during every decade of its existence. But whereas Israel was once perceived as being at the center of a boiling cauldron, many now seen it as a relative oasis of peace in an increasingly turbulent region. This view led former prime minister Ehud Barak to describe his country in somewhat belligerent terms as "a villa in the jungle"—and has partially driven the huge increase in barrier building.

For the moment, Israel is fairly stable—at least in comparison to the rest of the Middle East. In recent years, as the Arab world has been convulsed with revolutions and conflict, the spotlight has not been shining on Israel. However, the Israelis know this will change. Hezbollah, Hamas, and many other groups and organizations have not finished with Israel. The situation is fragile, and it doesn't take much to reignite the conflict, as we saw at the end of 2017 when President Trump officially recognized Jerusalem as Israel's capital, sparking unrest throughout the region. For the moment, all sides are building for the future. The walls are containing the violence—for now.

CHAPTER 4

The Middle East

Choose a leader who will invest in building bridges, not walls. Books, not weapons. Morality, not corruption.

—*Rise Up and Salute the Sun:*
The Writings of Suzy Kassem

Previous pages: A route leading to the fortified Green Zone area in Baghdad, Iraq, 2016.

S mall walls are all over the Middle East. Each one is a testament to the terrorist violence now endemic there. You can
see them in Baghdad, Damascus, Amman, Sana'a, Beirut,
Cairo, Riyadh—indeed, in almost every capital city. These concrete
barriers and blast walls have sprung up around embassies, charity
headquarters, international organizations, police stations, army
barracks, government buildings, housing compounds, churches,
hotels, and even whole neighborhoods.

On one side is normal life, car horns hooting, street vendors
hawking their goods, pedestrians going about the business of a
busy capital city; on the other is a version of normal life, with office
workers, government officials, civil servants, diplomats. They too
are going about their daily routine, but in the knowledge that
without the concrete blocks outside their windows, the guards
at the entrances to the premises, and possibly a checkpoint at
the end of the street, at any moment a truck bomb could bring
down their building, or a group of terrorists could burst into their
place of work.

It is no idle threat. The list of attacks that came before the
walls went up is long. In the wider Middle East more than 150
have occurred this century, including at compounds in Riyadh
housing foreign workers; hotels across Egypt's Sinai province
and in Jordan's Amman; oil facilities in Yemen and Algeria;
churches in Baghdad; the US consulate in Benghazi; the Bardo
Museum in Tunis; and the Iranian parliament and shrine of
Ayatollah Khomeini.

The walls went up in these at-risk urban centers in response to the many attacks. The template for this type of wall construction was the Green Zone in Baghdad, whose perimeter was built after the 2003 invasion of Iraq to protect the American-led provisional government in the post-Saddam years. Constituting a huge area of central Baghdad, the Green Zone was ringed by giant concrete slabs, similar to those we see in the walled section of the West Bank. In the Green Zone you got used to hearing explosions from rockets landing within the perimeter, but a more frequent sound was the distant dull thud of a mass-casualty car-bomb explosion or suicide attack on the outside, a constant reminder of what life was like for ordinary Iraqis and the American troops in the real world.

Some of the main roads leading from the airport to the Green Zone were lined with concrete blocks in a bid to prevent roadside bombs. As the threat grew, so did the extension of the blocks to secondary routes. They became so common that the US military had official names for the different types. They were named after US states: a Colorado was medium-size, at six feet tall and three and a half tons; the Texas was large, at six feet eight inches and six tons; and the Alaska came in at twelve feet and seven tons. The barriers saved lives, but were far from foolproof against "shaped" roadside bombs, which projected the force of a blast in one direction and could penetrate some walls. The barriers were costly, in blood and treasure; each block cost more than $600. Multiply that by thousands and eight years of occupation—the financial cost was in the billions.

Nevertheless, the walls came to be part of fighting an urban war, and building them an inherent part of America's military planning. Soldiers became adept at the skills required and could put up over a hundred blocks in a single night, sometimes under fire. As religious tensions between the Sunni and Shia populations grew and were deliberately exacerbated by militias on both sides, whole neighborhoods began to be walled off. The concrete saved lives, reducing the ability of the Sunni and Shia militias to get at civilian populations and foreign workers, but each slab was like a headstone and played its part in burying the idea that overthrowing Saddam would result in a stable Iraq.

Instead, the invasion of Iraq contributed to the destabilization of several countries, the growth of violent Islamist ideology, and eventually the creation of a vast lawless space from which violence was projected in all directions. The subsequent Arab uprisings that started in 2011 in Tunisia, Egypt, and Libya (which many wrongly called the Arab Spring, expecting that it would lead to large-sale reform across the region) may well have occurred anyway—we can never know. But when they did happen, each country had a coterie of jihadists trained in Iraq.

Many people used to believe that solving the Israeli/Palestinian issue would result in greater stability in the wider region, but that theory has been blown apart by the convulsions of the Arab world over the last few years. Now, with the conflicts in Iraq, Libya, Syria, Egypt, and Yemen, we have seen that the instability across the region has little to do with the situation in Gaza City, Ramallah, Tel Aviv, and Haifa.

In 2014 just 5 percent of the global population lived in the Arab world, but they suffered 45 percent of the world's terrorist attacks, 68 percent of global conflict–related deaths, and housed 58 percent of its refugees. Some countries have fallen apart; in others the cracks are showing; and in still others the divisions are hidden beneath the surface and could reappear at any moment. The wars and uprisings have laid bare the huge rifts in the Arab-dominated countries. A sense of Arab unity remains as they share a space, a language, and, to an extent, a religion; but pan-Arab unification remains a distant dream.

Religion is one of the biggest divisive factors. In 2004 King Abdullah of Jordan coined a controversial phrase when speaking about a "Shia crescent." He was referring to the expansion of Iranian influence, following an arc from Shia Iran's capital, Tehran, running through the now Shia-dominated Iraq capital, Baghdad, on to Damascus in Syria, where the ruling Assad family is descended from a Shia offshoot sect (Alawites), and ending in the Shia Hezbollah stronghold of south Beirut in Lebanon. This was highly unusual language in a region in which everyone knew that sectarian tensions existed, but preferred not to highlight them. King Abdullah was aware of the risks of sectarianism, however. In a 2007 newspaper interview, four years before the war in Syria broke out, he gave a prescient warning of what might be coming: "If sectarianism deepens and spreads, its destructive effect will reflect on everyone. It will foster division, polarization, and isolationism. Our region will drown in a conflict whose outcome cannot be foreseen."

The Sunni/Shia split within Islam has been present since the seventh century and thus is almost as old as the religion itself. The schism was about who should lead Islam after the death of Muhammad in 632. The Shi'at Ali, or "partisans of Ali," are what we now call the Shias. They held that leadership had to remain in Muhammad's family line and supported his cousin and son-in-law Ali ibn Abi Talib as caliph. What we now call Sunnis are those who disagreed, arguing that leadership should come from learned men within the community. They prevailed after killing one of Ali's sons, Hussein, at the Battle of Karbala (680) in what is now Iraq.

Ever since, each tradition holds that the other is not the true way of Islam; the Shias, for example, only recognize religious leaders who they say are descended from the Prophet through Ali and Hussein. Fast-forward fourteen hundred years and that difference is now manifest in many small but, to the believer, important ways that mark one sect from the other.

None of this is Koranic law, but just as everywhere else in the world, as the centuries pass and communities group together in separate neighborhoods, differences grow—and small differences in daily life can be writ large when it comes to politics. The names given to children are mostly not exclusive to one side or the other, but generalizations can be made. For example, it's unlikely someone named Yazid would be Shia, as Yazid is said to be the man who killed Hussein. In some countries the way a person dresses or the length of a man's beard would suggest whether the person was Sunni or Shia, and when you enter the homes of religious families, you can see paintings and posters indicating which sect they adhere to. The Sunni and Shia clerics wear different garb—it is unusual, but not impossible, to see a Sunni cleric wearing a black turban. The manner of praying also differs: Sunnis tend to fold their arms at times in the service when the Shias have their arms by their sides.

The majority of Arabs are Sunnis, but the Shias are a majority in Iran, Iraq, and Bahrain, and they form a substantial minority in Lebanon, Yemen, Kuwait, and Saudi Arabia, where they are concentrated in the east of the country. What unites the two sects—belief in the Five Pillars of Islam—is usually enough for them to live in peaceful coexistence, but those who find themselves in a minority do sometimes complain that they are being discriminated against and are shut out of government and other aspects of public life. Periods of tension have always at times led to sustained outbreaks of violence at both the local and regional levels. We are living through one such outbreak now.

In the Saddam era, Iraq was dominated by the minority Sunni population, but after he was overthrown, Shia groups became more powerful; militias on both sides have carried out multiple bombings and shootings to further their political aims. Iraq suffers from more terrorist attacks than any other country—nearly three thousand incidents in 2016, with over nine thousand dead—

the Islamic State (IS) being responsible for the worst of them. Having originated in Iraq following the 2003 US invasion, IS became one of the most notorious and widespread terror organizations, extending its presence across the Middle East, including Syria, Libya, Yemen, and Egypt. Most governments in the region are aware that IS could filter into and destabilize other areas with its extremist views and violent activities and are keen to prevent that from happening.

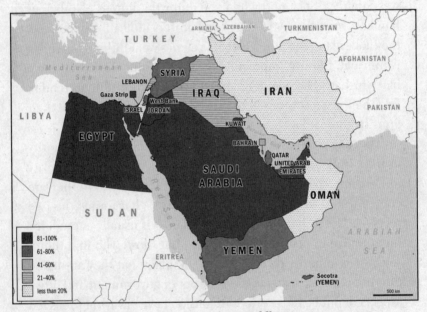

Proportion of Sunni Muslims across Middle Eastern countries.

In Yemen, civil war broke out in 2005 between rebel Shia Houthi forces and the Sunni-led government, with Iran backing the Houthis while Saudi Arabia, among others, supports the Sunni groups; both IS and al-Qaeda have also been active in the conflict. The violence intensified and spread across the country after 2015, killing thousands and displacing over 3 million. By

November 2017, the situation was described as "the world's worst humanitarian crisis" by UNICEF, exacerbated by widespread famine and cholera outbreaks.

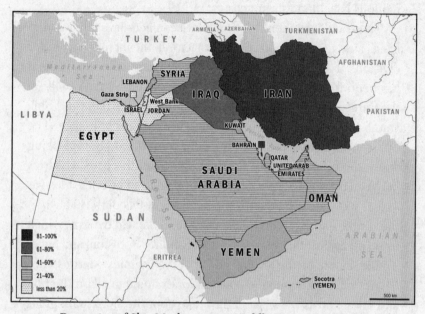

Proportion of Shia Muslims across Middle Eastern countries.

Syria has split along mostly sectarian and ethnic lines: Sunni, Shia, Alawi, Kurd, Christian, Druze, and so on. President Assad's father, Hafez, had bound the country together under a vicious secular dictatorship, but once the violence began in 2011, those shackles were quickly cast off. The civil war in Syria is one of the most violent and complicated conflicts in the world, with multiple players involved (including foreign military intervention from Russia, Turkey, the USA, and others). Iran backs the Assad regime, while Saudi Arabia supports some of the Sunni rebel groups. IS has again had a major role in the conflict, although by the end of 2017 it had lost almost all the territory it had previously gained in both Syria and Iraq. Atrocities have been committed by all sides; the government has even been accused of using chemical weapons against its own people. As a result of the widespread violence, millions have been displaced within the country, and millions have fled as refugees.

These and the other Middle Eastern conflicts have other underlying causes, but religion is a major factor in the increasingly bitter divisions. The split between Sunni and Shia is wider now than it has been for centuries. This is partially driven by state politics: the fierce regional rivalry between Sunni Saudi Arabia and Shia Iran has exacerbated the problem as both vie for influence. The differences between them also stem from ethnicity, one being Arab, the other majority Persian, and from the usual rivalries between powerful states, but the language used by both sides has a clear sectarian edge. Hard-line Sunnis now talk of the Safawis— the Arabic name for the Persian (Iranian) Safavid dynasty, which faced off against the Sunni Ottoman Empire. Both Iran and Saudi Arabia want to be the leading power of the Islamic countries; they have conflicting economic policies, for example in oil production and sales, and as we've seen, they take opposite sides in religious conflicts that break out in other countries across the region. Both have also accused each other of supporting terrorist groups and their activities. In response, across the Middle East and North Africa, this era of division is giving way to an age of walls.

Saudi Arabia has built hundreds of miles of fence along its northern and southern borders, Kuwait has fenced off its frontiers, and Jordan has fortified its border with Syria; to the north the Turks have built a wall ten feet high and seven feet thick along its border with Syria, while the convulsions in Libya have led Tunisia and Egypt to construct fences along their frontiers.

The barrier building in Jordan is the most technologically impressive, even if the reasons for it are the most depressing. The wars in Syria to its north and Iraq to its east have resulted in hundreds of thousands of refugees flooding into the country. The Hashemite Kingdom began shoring up its defenses in 2008, aware that the violence and chaos in Iraq might spread. This was three years before the Syrian war broke out, but even then, the region's instability and the growth in international terrorism induced the Obama administration to offer assistance to its ally. At first the initiative was modest, with plans to build watchtowers along a sensitive thirty-mile stretch of the Syrian border sometimes used by smugglers. As Syria descended into chaos and IS threatened to bring its terror into Jordan, the project expanded, as did the cost. Jordan is 95 percent Sunni, and IS intended to promote its extreme beliefs in a fragile and religious country.

Washington, DC, funded the Jordan Border Security Program out of the Pentagon's Defense Threat Reduction Agency (DTRA), the Raytheon company being awarded most of the contract. A 160-mile-long high-tech security fence along the Syrian frontier now has watchtowers, night-vision cameras, and ground sensors that can detect movement five miles from each side of the border. A similar structure covers 115 miles of the Iraq border. The DTRA's website says the world "can be downright scary" and notes the use of WMDs in both Syria and Iraq. Its work on the fence, it says, "is a great example of how we are Making the World Safer from weapons of mass destruction."

What it doesn't say is that the barrier is also helping to keep American military personnel in Jordan safer. Officially, only a few dozen US military personnel are based in Jordan; in reality there are usually at least several hundred, but they work mostly out of sight on Jordanian military bases. These fictional low numbers can be sustained in official documents so long as those in the country are "deployed" and not "based" there. Jordan may be an American ally, but the government prefers not to be seen as too close to the superpower to avoid inflaming anti-American sentiment among the minority of its population considered to be Islamists.

The border fences constructed by the Saudis are even longer, and costlier, than those in Jordan, but they were also built with American assistance. The Northern Border Project covers over 550 miles of the Iraq frontier. It has a triple fence, a giant sand berm, thirty-two "response stations" linked to seven command-and-control centers, all backed up by 240 quick-response vehicles.

Relations between Saudi Arabia and Iraq are difficult. Many Iraqis blame Saudi Arabia for exporting its fierce interpretation of Sunni Islam and thus helping to create IS, which has caused so much bloodshed in their country; and since the overthrow of Saddam Hussein, a Shia-dominated Iraq has grown closer to Iran. However, in 2017, in an effort to draw Iraq away from Iran, Riyadh began a charm offensive and even invited high-profile Iraqi politicians to visit. Relations between the two countries have improved in recent years, but for now Iraq remains more closely aligned with Iran.

To its south Saudi Arabia has fenced off part of its border with Yemen. This project began in 2003 and, as with Jordan's original plan for the Syrian fence, was originally designed to reduce arms- and people-smuggling from dirt-poor Yemen into the far richer Saudi Arabia. At first the Saudis concentrated on stopping vehicles by placing sandbags and concrete blocks in the crossing areas in the mountainous terrain to the southwest. However, in 2009, after Shia Houthi rebels from Yemen staged a cross-border raid and killed two Saudi guards, Riyadh sanctioned the building of fences with electric sensors to prevent people from crossing on foot along a stretch of frontier about a hundred miles long. The Houthis' military campaign was aimed at achieving greater autonomy in Yemen, but on occasion it spilled across into Saudi Arabia's Jizan province, turning the Saudis against them. This hostility increased once the Saudis perceived that their main regional rival, Iran, was assisting the Houthis.

When Yemen's civil war broke out, al-Qaeda strengthened its position in the country and used it as a launching pad to move people into Saudi Arabia. So now Saudi Arabia had the triple problem of Shia Houthi fighters and cross-border raids, migrants crossing illegally, and al-Qaeda, which has sworn to overthrow the royal family, all pressing up against its southern frontier; so the fence was deemed even more necessary. The fence still leaves hundreds of miles of the border open in the desert areas to the east, but here the distances are so great, and the conditions so brutal, that it is harder to evade patrols and there are fewer crossings.

As well as the problems along its borders, Saudi Arabia is also aware of the threat of internal division. Although the country is utterly dominated by Sunnis, with Shias composing at most 15 percent of a population of 33 million, that minority is largely concentrated in the eastern provinces, where most of Saudi Arabia's oil fields are located. The Shia-dominated provinces are growing restless: they say that their communities are grossly underfunded and that they are shut out of national life—charges the government denies. Given this potential source of trouble, the ongoing instability of Yemen, and the fractures in Iraq, Saudi Arabia is in no mood to consider tearing down the barriers it has put up and constantly looks for ways to improve them.

Kuwait is also keen to maintain a buffer between it and Iraq, despite the fall of Saddam Hussein in 2003, as the two countries have a long history of conflict. Kuwait was established as a sheikdom in the Anglo-Ottoman Convention of 1913, but Iraq's governments have never accepted what are essentially British-drawn borders and have at various times claimed the oil-rich state as its nineteenth province.

Iraqi forces invaded Kuwait in 1990 but were driven out by a US-led coalition. Kuwait then constructed, literally, a line in the sand between the two countries. A six-mile-deep barrier consisting of three parallel sand berms arose along the entire length of the border. Parts were topped with barbed wire and had tank ditches in front of them. It was meant to keep the Iraqis out, but in 2003, during the next US-led invasion, the Americans had to cross the hurdle to get in. This major operation required breaching the berm in several places simultaneously and at such speed that the defending Iraqis couldn't attack columns of single-file vehicles and halt the advance in its tracks. The Americans pulled it off, and ten thousand vehicles came through, most heading, ultimately, for Baghdad.

The following year, Iraq may no longer have been a strategic threat to Kuwait, but the Kuwaitis still wanted a new, better barrier between them. Under UN legal supervision, a location was agreed upon by both sides, and a 135-mile-long fence has since been erected from the Iraqi border town of Umm Qasr to the border triangle where Iraq, Kuwait, and Saudi Arabia meet. Like so many other countries in the Middle East, Kuwait is trying to guard itself against the proliferating violence in Iraq and also stop illegal immigration into its much wealthier economy.

Turkey, meanwhile, is more concerned about the threat posed by Syria and is building a wall along part of the border. It is supplemented by trenches, a floodlighting system, watchtowers, surveillance balloons, thermal imaging, radar, a targeting system, and small armored vehicles called Cobra IIs, which drive along the wall using cameras mounted on angled cranes to peer over the top. Having sided with the opposition to Assad and taken an active role in the conflict, Turkey is now trying to stop refugees and terrorists entering from Syria. But Turkey has another concern in the Syria conflict, and that is the growing strength of Kurdish groups taking part in it.

When we talk about the Middle East, we often think of "the Arabs" as if they are interchangeable, or a monolith, whereas in fact the region is home to numerous peoples, religions, sects, and languages, with minorities such as the Kurds, the Druze, the Yazidis, and Chaldeans.

The Kurds are the biggest minority, with about 30 million in the Middle East. Estimates vary, but suggest about 2 million are in Syria, 6 million in Iraq, 6 million in Iran, and 15 million in Turkey. It's often said they are the world's largest nation without a state, although the Tamils in Sri Lanka and India might argue with that. The national subdivisions of the Kurds are further divided into about a hundred tribes that adhere to different religious sects and speak a number of languages, which are also split into different dialects and alphabets or scripts.

While a movement seeks to create a nation-state of Kurdistan, the Kurdish people, given their differences, geographical locations, and the opposition of existing states, are unlikely to be unified by one state. The Turkish military incursion into northern Syria in early 2018 was mostly to split Kurdish forces and ensure a mini statelet could not be formed out of the wreckage of Syria. The 2017 nonbinding referendum in Iraqi Kurdistan, backing independence, was supposed to be a step toward the great Kurdish dream, but Turkey and Iran will not permit a united Kurdistan that includes an inch of their own territories. In Iraq, the central government responded to the independence vote by sending in the army to seize the Kurdish-controlled oil city of Kirkuk with the message that neither plans for independence nor expansion out of traditionally Kurdish-dominated areas would be permitted. Within Iraq the Kurds are split into two tribal configurations, with similar splits in other areas. The Kurds suffer discrimination within the countries they find themselves split among. Those in Iraq have particularly bad memories of Saddam Hussein's "socialist" Ba'ath Party. It gassed thousands of them during the brutal Anfal military campaign of the 1980s, and killed thousands more in the following decade.

This brutal authoritarianism wasn't at all unusual for governments across the Middle East, and many—not just the Kurds—have suffered the consequences.

What went wrong in the Arab world? Just about everything. What has been tried as a solution to the problem? Just about everything.

Many reasons are given for the problem. Religion, for example, has caused great rifts, as we have seen. Colonialism resulted in the creation of nation-states whose boundaries ignored traditional cultural divisions—peoples who once thought of themselves as different, and who had been governed differently, were now expected to pledge loyalty to an entity some felt they had little in common with, while others who had previously identified as a single community were split down the middle. The geography of the region provided most areas with little natural wealth, and not all those blessed—or, depending on your view, cursed—with oil shared its profits equitably. What wealth there is often seems to be squandered by the elite, and poverty and a general lack of economic and social progress are widespread.

The Arab Human Development Report 2002, written by a group of eminent Arab intellectuals led by the Egyptian statistician Nader Fergany and sponsored by the United Nations Development Programme, best summed up the situation for the twenty-two Arab countries. The report noted that education levels and life expectancy were up, and child mortality rates down, but that was just about the sum total of the positives. The authors removed from their statistics a traditional measure of success, income per head, on the grounds that the massive energy wealth of a few countries, which trickled down to only a few people, skewed the numbers. They then added internet access and freedom levels to create the Alternative Human Development Index. In a cutting sentence they concluded, "The region is richer than it is it developed."

In particular, they highlighted what they called the Three Deficits that were holding the region back. First, because it lacked certain freedoms, the Arab world had failed to keep up with global knowledge in science, political thought, and comparative religion. Relatively few books translated from languages other than Arabic are freely available across the region. Second, and related to this, was the failure to embrace developments in communications in order to disseminate what knowledge was available. Third, women's participation in politics and work was the lowest in the world.

The lack of civil rights and freedom of speech and the blatant censorship in most Arab countries meant that, despite reasonable spending on education, the money was misused, and the results were poor. The report said that in the past one thousand years fewer books have been translated into Arabic than are translated into Spanish in Spain in one year. Internet use was restricted to just 0.6 percent of the population.

A generation of progressive Arab intellectuals and politicians took the report as a wake-up call, but progressives are a minority in the Arab world, and not enough were in positions of authority to bring about change. Almost twenty years on, things are worse. By 2016, according to the UN's Arab Development Report, internet penetration had massively increased to above 50 percent, but overall the Three Deficits were still holding the region back. Arab regimes remained ruthlessly aggressive against dissent, individual liberties were still curtailed, many of the ideas of the outside world continued to be unwelcome, and eleven Arab countries were suffering internal conflicts.

Many Arab secularists blame the problems and lack of freedom on what is sometimes referred to as "the closing of the Arab mind." This refers to the ending of the practice of *ijtihad*. The direct translation of the word is "effort," but it means the interpretation of religious problems not precisely covered by the Koran or the hadith—the reports of what the Prophet Muhammad did and said. For several centuries any learned Muslim scholar could come up with original thinking on religious questions, but by the end of the Sunni Abbasid caliphate (750–1258), it was declared that the gates of *ijtihad* were closed. The laws and interpretations laid down by the great men of previous generations were not to be questioned.

Some argue that this "closure" has held the Arab world back, and in modern times it has become one of the great divides within Arab societies between those seeking reform and those holding firm to tradition. If this theory is true, it would go some way to explaining why other cultures, which share a lack of freedoms and human rights, have developed and challenged Western countries in technology and economic progress; Singapore and China come to mind. Arab culture *is* deeply respectful of tradition and authority, and less open to change than that of many other regions. One man seemingly trying to change this is the new crown prince of Saudi Arabia, Mohammed bin Salman (widely referred to as MbS). In what appears to be a carefully thought-out plan, the king of Saudi Arabia, Salman bin Abdulaziz Al Saud, bestowed the title of crown prince and significant powers upon his thirty-two-year-old son. Both men appear to have concluded that the kingdom will not survive with its current economic base and societal norms. The crown prince unveiled his Vision 2030 economic model, diversifying the economy away from its reliance on energy. Part of this was the hugely controversial reform to allow women to drive by the middle of 2018, as he realized a modern economy cannot ignore 50 percent of its workforce. As 2017 ended, he followed this up with a purge of hard-liners. The crown prince, along with other Gulf State allies such as Abu Dhabi's crown prince Mohammed bin Zayed Al Nahyan, is trying to break out of the traditional straitjacket but knows he must tread carefully. In this they are mostly supported by the younger generations in their societies.

Politically, the Arabs have tried nationalism and faux socialism, and they have experienced the strong leader. Life under jihadist rule in the shape of IS is another failed system, while some live under the hereditary power of royal families. Of all these regimes the latter has tended to be the most stable and, starting from a shockingly low base, relatively benign, but no system the Arabs have yet tried has succeeded in uniting them in a successful nation-state at peace with itself, nor as a region, despite the unifying factor of language.

The great dream of a united Arabia was evident in the proclamations of the 1916 Arab Revolt. But it was only ever a dream, and the divides between its peoples almost certainly mean it will never be realized. The Arab professor Fawaz Gerges admits that the outlook is gloomy: "Time and again Arab rulers battle each other for influence and power and frequently interfere in the affairs of each other. . . . These fierce rivalries have had debilitating effects on the Arab state system and have caused mayhem and civil wars. The system is broken."

With no solid democratic platform upon which to build, the Arab nation-states have failed to gain the loyalty of the majority of their peoples. As the 2016 UN report says, "Young people are gripped by an inherent sense of discrimination and exclusion," thus leading to a "weakening [of] their commitment to preserving government institutions."

We've seen the cracks appear in the edifice of the European Union, where they are leading to a partial retreat into nationalism. The difference in the Middle East is that the Arabs are less rooted in the concept of the nation-state and have not fully embraced ideas about individual liberty; therefore, when government institutions break down, many people retreat to the precursors of the nation-state—religion, ethnicity, and the tribe.

As the Sunnis, the Shias, and the tribes and ethnicities withdraw behind their physical and psychological walls and the nation-states weaken, their religion offers them self-respect, identity, and certainty. On this basis the Islamists can construct a worldview according to which socialism, nationalism, or even the nation-state itself is a cancer and that Islam is the answer. They build ideological barriers around themselves that become so high that those behind them can no longer see beyond them. Thus imprisoned in narrow minds, some come to see the "other" as infidel (*kafir*), unbeliever, Safawi, worthy only of being subjugated or killed. Once immured, it is hard to ever come back.

One explanation for this is poverty and poor education. Neither factor can be ignored; however, too much importance is attached to them, giving rise to the belief that if you eradicate poverty and improve education, you eradicate Islamist ideology. This does not take into account the huge numbers of highly educated jihadists, whose ranks are each year swollen by university graduates, especially those with engineering degrees. Nor does it explain why some of the most violent ideology springs from the richest country in the region—Saudi Arabia. Without question, better living standards and higher-quality secular education are part of the solution, but ironically, another wall is needed here, the one built in most successful modern societies—that between religion and politics.

Because Islam is an all-encompassing way of life, many practitioners find it difficult to take religion and ethnicity out of politics. There is nothing in the Koran along the lines attributed to Jesus—"Render to Caesar the things that are Caesar's; and to God the things that are God's." Without this disconnection, religious law tends to underpin or even dominate secular law, and the prevailing religion or sect will ensure that its version of religion and law is the one adhered to.

In contrast, in Europe the formation and organization of political parties along ethnic or religious lines has largely been eradicated. Most political parties attract support across wide and varied sections of society, and religion doesn't play much of a role in government and policy making.

However, in the Middle East, memories of "secular politics" are those of despotic rule—the Ba'ath Party of Syria and Iraq are examples. Both pretended to be secular socialist parties above ethnic and religious divides, but both brutally suppressed their populations. This has led some people to mistrust the ability of secular parties to defend their interests, and they turn instead to the party that supports their religion.

For now the Arab countries and peoples remain divided and ravaged by conflict, both within and between countries. The Saudis and Iranians play out a geopolitical regional battle that, when it reaches the local level, manifests itself in the ancient Shia/Sunni rift, which in turn also plays out in conflicts beyond their own borders. So many of the conflicts across the region—such as the war in Iraq—allowed similar fissures to surface, with the ensuing violence and extremism rippling across borders. Caught up in the maelstrom are minorities such as the Christians, Yazidis, and Druze.

The dream of pan-Arab unity has turned into the nightmare of pan-Arab divisions. Once these sectarian demons are unleashed, the suspicion and fear of the "other" take years, sometimes generations, to be reversed. The patchwork quilt of nation-states such as Syria has been ripped up, and the design pattern of any future states is still unclear. A generation of young, educated, urban Arabs are seeking to put the divisions behind them, but the weight of history holds them back.

The Egyptian president Anwar Sadat said the following words in a speech at the Israeli Knesset in 1977, referring to the Arab-Israeli conflict; but more than forty years on they still apply, right across the region: "Yet, there remains another wall. This wall constitutes a psychological barrier between us; a barrier of suspicion; a barrier of rejection; a barrier of fear, of deception; a barrier of hallucination without any action, deed, or decision."

CHAPTER 5

The Indian Subcontinent

Like all walls it was ambiguous, two faced. What was inside it and what was outside it depended upon which side you were on.

—Ursula K. Le Guin,
The Dispossessed

On India's frontier with Bangladesh is the longest border fence in the world. It runs along most of the twenty-five-hundred-mile boundary that India wraps around its much smaller neighbor; the only part of Bangladesh completely free of it is its 360-mile-long coast at the Bay of Bengal. The fence zigzags from the bay northward, along mostly flattish ground, up toward the more hilly country near Nepal and Bhutan, takes a right turn along the top of the country, then drops down south again, often through heavily forested areas, back to the sea. It passes through plains and jungle, beside rivers and over hills. The territories on each side are heavily populated, and in many areas the ground is cultivated as close to the barrier as possible, which means the crops grown often touch the divide.

Hundreds of miles of this barrier are double layered, parts of it are barbed wire, parts are walled, parts electrified, and parts floodlit. In some stretches, West Bengal, for example, which comprises about half the border length, the fence is fitted with smart sensors, direction finders, thermal-imaging equipment, and night-vision cameras connected to a satellite-based signal command system.

The Indians are trying to move from a system that relied on large numbers of troops patrolling long stretches of border almost constantly to one that can easily pinpoint breaches in the fence and dispatch quick-reaction units. As with other frontiers around the world, technology has simplified what would previously have taken hundreds of man-hours to monitor, report, and act swiftly upon. Even if a sensor is tripped miles away from a control room, within a minute a drone can be overhead and a patrol on its way; the technology becomes more sophisticated each year.

Despite these measures, the Indian fence fails to stop people from trying to cross. They continue to do so despite the barbed wire, and despite border guards having shot dead hundreds of people attempting to get into India, and many others wanting to return to Bangladesh surreptitiously after being in India illegally. Among them, in 2011, was fifteen-year-old Felani Khatun.

Felani's family had been working illegally in India without passports or visas, due to the legal complexity and costs of obtaining either. To return home for a family visit Felani and her father had paid a smuggler $50 to get them across. Just after dawn, with the border fence shrouded in mist, she began climbing a bamboo ladder placed against it by the smuggler. Her *shalwar kameez* snagged on the barbed wire. She panicked and began to shout to her father for help. Following a number of terrorist infiltrations, India's Border Security Force (BSF) were under orders to shoot to kill, and a border guard followed orders. It was a slow death. She remained dangling on the fence, bleeding but still alive, for several hours. As the sun rose and the mist lifted, she could be seen and heard crying out for water before finally succumbing to her wounds. The shockingly violent, drawn-out death of such a young girl drew international attention and condemnation at the shoot-to-kill policy. Inevitably attention waned, but the politics remain, and so does the fence. Her death stands as testimony to the human cost of such barriers. India is not unique in this; there has been an increase in such deaths around the world. Dr. Reece Jones points out that "2016 set the record for border deaths (7,200 globally) because of the increase in border security."

The fence on India's border with Bangladesh is justified as preventing weapons- and contraband-smuggling and deterring cross-border insurgents; but primarily it's there to prevent illegal immigration at levels that have resulted in riots and the mass killing of foreigners. Its main purpose is to keep people out. But in this turbulent region, migration is not the only issue. The divisions across the subcontinent, as we find so often around the world, stem partially from borders drawn by colonial powers, compounded by regional religious and ethnic prejudice and political realities. Many of the religious rifts can be traced back to Muslim rule over India in medieval times.

Following the first Islamic invasions from Central Asia, masses of the predominantly Hindu population converted; but the sheer size of India created problems for the invaders. As with China, it is almost impossible for an outside power to fully control India without building alliances. So although tens of millions of people converted to Islam, that still left hundreds of millions as Hindus. Even under the Mughal dynasty (1526–1857), when Muslim power expanded over almost all of India, the conquerors realized what the British would later discover: to take advantage of the subcontinent's riches, it was easier to divide and rule the various regions than to seek absolute power. West of the Thar Desert and in the Ganges delta, a majority of people converted to Islam (the same regions that now compose Pakistan and Bangladesh), but almost everywhere else the majority of people remained Hindu.

In 1947, as the British withdrew, India's founding fathers, especially Mahatma Gandhi, envisioned creating a multifaith democratic state stretching east to west from the Hindu Kush to the Rakhine Mountains, and north to south from the Himalayas to the Indian Ocean. But Mohammed Ali Jinnah, who would go on to become Pakistan's first leader, believed that because Muslims would be a minority in this state, they required their own country. He wanted "a Muslim country for Muslims" and helped invent a border that was partially drawn along religious, not geographical, lines. The borders were drawn—by the British—to separate off areas that had a mainly Muslim population. So in 1947 two states came into being, India and Pakistan, the latter comprising West and East Pakistan. The religious divisions had become geographical ones, marked in the mind and on the landscape.

But often the border bisected existing communities, and all areas were mixed to some degree, so many people were compelled to move. The great division of the subcontinent in 1947 was accompanied by a wild bout of bloodletting. Millions were killed during the mass movement of peoples as Sikhs, Hindus, and Muslims headed for regions where they would feel safe. Psychologically, none of the countries involved have ever recovered; the divides between them are as great as ever and are now increasingly manifested in concrete and barbed wire.

India is a magnet for migrants. It is a democracy, laws protect minorities, and compared to its neighbors, it has a thriving economy. Refugees and illegal immigrants have flocked there from Afghanistan, Sri Lanka, Myanmar (formerly known as Burma), Tibet, Pakistan, and Bangladesh. At least 110,000 Tibetans have fled since China annexed their territory in 1951, around 100,000 Tamil Sri Lankans arrived during their island's civil war that ended earlier this century, and the upheavals in Afghanistan have led to a steady flow of people to India. But by far the greatest number of immigrants are from Bangladesh, which is surrounded by India on three sides.

Since the partition of India in 1947 waves of people from what was then East Pakistan have crossed into India to escape persecution, intolerance, and economic hardship, but the number increased following the violent conflict with West Pakistan. A glance at the map quickly shows why the two were never destined to remain a single country. They are thirteen hundred miles apart with different geographics and linguistics. After years of discrimination from West Pakistan, in 1971 the Bengalis in East Pakistan started agitating for independence. The Pakistani government

ruthlessly attempted to suppress them, and in the ensuing violence, in which millions were killed, millions also fled to India.
Today, many thousands are thought to cross the border every year.

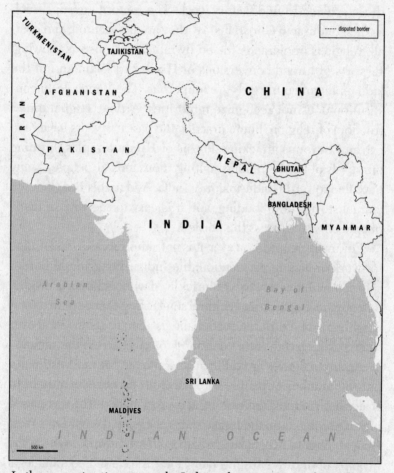

In the mass migrations across the Indian subcontinent, people are fleeing
poverty, the effects of climate change, and religious persecution.

Life is hard for many in Bangladesh. Around 12.9 percent of
the population live below the national poverty line, as defined

by the Asian Development Bank. Huge inroads have been made
into the problem, but life remains extremely harsh for tens of
millions of people. In rural areas the work consists of backbreaking farm labor, and in the growing cities massive slums house
those arriving to find factory work. The minority groups, such
as the Hindus and Christians, say they are persecuted, and overall, religious intolerance fueled by radical Islamists is growing.
Reports of forced conversions of Hindus to Islam and of the
kidnapping of young girls are numerous. The Bangladeshi constitution does not recognize minorities. Article 41 guarantees
freedom of religion, but in practice the past few years have seen
extremist groups attacking dozens of Hindu temples, burning
hundreds of homes, and assaulting thousands of people. Many
have fled toward Hindu-majority India. Add to this Bangladesh's
annual storms and flooding, and it is easy to see why so many
people choose to cross the border.

For many people, however, it is not simply a case of migrating
for work or fleeing persecution: the Indian-Bangladeshi border
split communities that for centuries lived without physical divides.
Some share linguistic and cultural similarities—the idea that their
neighbor is of a different nationality is alien to them—and ever
since partition they have continued to travel across the region.

Accurate figures are difficult to come by, but most estimates
put the number of people who have moved permanently from
Bangladesh to India this century at over 15 million. This has caused
massive problems in the Indian states closest to the border—West
Bengal, Assam, Meghalaya, Mizoram, and Tripura—where the
majority of (mostly Muslim) Bangladeshis have settled, but illegal
Bangladeshi migrants are to be found in all the major cities of
India. One of the most affected states is Assam, in the northeast
of India. During the Bangladesh War of Independence the majority of people fleeing to India were Hindu, but soon increasingly
large numbers of Muslims joined them. Between 1971 and 1991

the Muslim population in Assam increased by 77 percent, from 3.5 million to 6.3 million, prompting a major ethnic backlash against them, with locals complaining that not only was pressure being put on jobs and housing, but also that their identity and culture were being challenged. Some Hindus fell prey to blaming all ills on the newcomers no matter what their background because they were not Assamese, but Muslims suffered the most. What are essentially small differences, say, in the eating of pork or beef, became magnified as tensions rose.

In 1982 mass anti-Bangladeshi demonstrations began in Assam, leading to the formation of militias and eventually to rioting, in which thousands of non-Assamese were slaughtered. Muslims were the main victims, but in many cases, again, people didn't bother to differentiate between ethnic or religious groups. Indira Gandhi responded with plans for a barbed-wire border fence, which the subsequent government of Rajiv Gandhi promised to implement.

Assam is useful in understanding the wider problems India faces. As elsewhere, Assam's terrain makes it almost impossible to secure the border fully. It shares only 163 miles of frontier with Bangladesh, but some of this is the Brahmaputra River, which floods each year and changes course, making it difficult to fix a permanent boundary marker.

Since 1971, Assam's population has more than doubled, from 14.6 million to over 30 million, much of which is due to illegal immigration. Hindu nationalists have argued that the area might have a Muslim majority by 2060. In 2015 there were 19 million Hindus and 11 million Muslims, nine of the twenty-seven districts being majority Muslim. Equally important, the 2017 census showed that people who are ethnically Assamese are now a minority in the state as a whole, and as people continue to arrive, that proportion will continue to drop.

After the murderous riots of 1982, parliament passed the Assam Accord in 1985, cosigned both by the national and state

governments and by the leaders of the violent movements that
had helped agitate the unrest three years earlier. The accord
was intended to reduce the number of migrants in the area and
referred back to the Pakistan war of 1971. Those who had arrived
before 1971 could stay on certain conditions, but all foreigners
who had entered Assam on or after March 25 of that year—the day
on which the Pakistani army began full-scale operations against
civilians—were to be traced and deported, as by 1985 Bangladesh
was considered to be sufficiently stable for refugees to return.

It didn't work. Of the 10 million who had fled Bangladesh
during the war, millions remained in India, and more kept coming.
As a result, over the years the fences have become longer, taller,
and increasingly high-tech. The central government has focused
on wall building rather than enforcing the accord and creating a
legal framework for a solution. All the while the human cost has
been rising: according to Human Rights Watch, in the first decade
of this century, BSF personnel gunned down an estimated nine
hundred Bangladeshis as they attempted to cross the border.

Most people willing to take the risk do make it into India. But
once there, they find themselves in a legal nightmare. India has
no effective national refugee or illegal-immigrant laws. It has not
signed the 1951 UN Refugee Convention on the grounds that
it doesn't take into consideration the complexities of regional
problems. Instead, all foreigners come under the 1946 Foreigners
Act, which defines a foreigner as "a person who is not a citizen
of India," which may have the benefit of succinctness but is of
limited use in deciding who is a genuine refugee, who qualifies
for asylum, and who is an economic migrant.

The ongoing problems—the resentment of the Indian population, the murky status of the immigrants themselves—highlight
the difficulties faced anywhere in the world when proper systems
aren't in place to deal with large population influxes, especially
when moving from one developing country to another.

Sanjeev Tripathi, the former head of India's foreign intelligence agency, the Research and Analysis Wing, argues that India needs a new law to define refugees and illegal immigrants. It must also come to an agreement with Bangladesh that Dhaka will take back Bangladeshis and issue them documents, and that "this would have to be followed by concerted action to detect Bangladeshi immigrants, assign them to separate categories of refugees and illegal migrants, resettle or repatriate them, and prevent any further influx." As he says, the current system has "substantially contributed to changing the demographic pattern in the north-eastern states of India, where the locals feel overwhelmed by the outsiders. This has adversely affected their way of life and led to simmering tension between the two sides."

The legal aspect of this is achievable through domestic political will; however, the diplomatic cooperation required from Bangladesh is more problematic. It not only prevaricates regarding the administrative paperwork sometimes required to take back migrants, but there are myriad stories of Bangladeshi guards pushing returning Bangladeshis back across the border into India, especially if they are from the Hindu minority.

An added problem is rounding up those deemed to be illegal. Millions of them are well embedded inside India; they often hold identity cards called Aadhaar, which do not distinguish them from Indian citizens for simple identification purposes, although they cannot be used to access all the facilities afforded an Indian citizen. Furthermore, in regions such as West Bengal the problem is compounded as the features and dialect of a Bangladeshi and a West Bengalese are hard to tell apart.

Another ongoing battle in Indian politics is over whether Bangladeshi Hindus should be granted citizenship on the grounds that they have fled persecution. When the Hindu nationalist Bharatiya Janata Party (BJP) gained power, it took this issue into account; after all, the 2014 party manifesto included, "India shall remain a natural home for persecuted Hindus and they shall be welcome to seek refuge here." However, the BJP has dragged its heels, well aware that although Muslim immigration is the greater concern for many voters in the border states, all outsiders face degrees of hostility.

Many supporters of the BJP government take a robust view of what is required and demand policies that might appear harsh to some people. These include criminal proceedings against anyone harboring an illegal immigrant, and banning illegal immigrants from working if they do not voluntarily register with the authorities. In the 2014 national election campaign Narendra Modi, the BJP leader, repeatedly promised that he would tighten border controls and warned illegal immigrants from Bangladesh that they needed to have their "bags packed." He went on to become prime minister.

In 2017 the BJP president, Amit Shah, accused politicians in the opposition Congress Party, who are against deportations, of wanting to make Assam a part of Bangladesh. Many in government see the problem in national security terms. Seen through the Indian security lens, the problem looks like this: Pakistan has never forgiven India for helping Bangladesh gain independence. To sow discord, it promotes a strategy known as "forward strategic depth." It encourages illegal immigration and sponsors cross-border terrorism from Bangladesh, supporting the activities of groups such as Harkat-ul-Jihad al-Islami and Jamaat-ul-Mujahideen Bangladesh and the movement of hundreds of their fighters into India. The theory continues that by changing the Hindu-Muslim demographics in Indian regions bordering Bangladesh, political parties will form that will demand autonomy and eventually independence, thus creating a new Muslim homeland. There is even a name for this imagined future state formed out of Assam and West Bengal: Bango Bhoomi. Thus, the theory concludes, India is weakened and Pakistan gains a foothold next to Bangladesh.

Those who think such a plan exists struggle to find hard evidence of it, but point to the changing demographics to bolster their argument. State-to-state relations between India and Bangladesh are cordial, but the fraught internal politics of the postpartition subcontinent, of Hindu and Muslim nationalisms, means that politicians often pander to the emotions of identity.

Whether or not the Bango Bhoomi theory is true, many nongovernment experts in border control argue that walls and fences are of limited use in preventing the flow of people, and that they are especially ineffective in combating terrorism. Dr. Reece Jones says that despite the vast sums spent on building the new high-tech India-Bangladesh fence, it "likely has no impact" on terrorist infiltration because "a terrorist often has the funds to pay for fake documents and simply cross the border at checkpoints or travel with valid documents." He also observes, "The threat of terrorism is used to justify walls, but the underlying issue is almost always unauthorized movement by the poor." Talk of Bango Bhoomi is not welcomed in Bangladesh, which views the Indian fence building as arrogant, aggressive, and damaging to the countries' relationship.

Many Bangladeshis feel hemmed in: to their east, west, and north is the Indian fence, and to their south, the Bay of Bengal, the sea. And the sea is getting closer every year.

Bangladesh is one of the most densely populated countries in the world. It is smaller than the US state of Florida but is home to 165 million people, compared to Florida's 21 million, and the population is growing rapidly. Most of the country is situated at sea level on the Ganges delta. It has hundreds of rivers, many of which flood each year, displacing millions of people. Most of them do eventually return to their land as the waters subside; however, many climate experts predict that within eighty years there will be at least a 2°C rise in land temperature and a three-foot rise in sea level. If that happens, a fifth of Bangladesh will disappear under the waves. Some of the areas most at risk are in the coastal regions that abut India such as Khulna, Satkhira, and Bagerhat, but around 80 percent of the country lies just above sea level.

Bangladesh contains hundreds of rivers, and much
of the land is at risk of flooding.

Upriver, reduced glacial melt from the Himalayas has already turned some of Bangladesh's precious fertile land into desert. This is expected to continue and is driving hundreds of thousands of people from the rural areas into the cities, sometimes simply to find fresh water after their supplies are contaminated by the sea encroaching into the rivers. The rapidly growing urban areas are ill prepared to accommodate them. The International Organization for Migration estimates that 70 percent of Dhaka's slum population arrived in the capital because of environmental disasters such as flooding or hurricanes.

Many parts of the world are already seeing "climate refugees," and tens of millions more are destined to be, heading mostly for urban areas, as even small changes to climate can have catastrophic results for local populations. In Africa, for example, droughts over the last few decades have created severe famine in many regions, while the Sahara Desert is also expanding slowly southward. But in Asia, climate refugees are mostly trying to escape floods. A 2010 study published by the London School of Economics suggests that of the top ten coastal cities most exposed to flooding, nine were in Asia. Dhaka was third behind Kolkata and Mumbai.

When you apply this predicted future to a country such as Bangladesh, where modern health care is scarce and education levels low, if a fifth of the land is flooded, and some of the rest is no longer fit for agriculture, then obviously huge numbers of people will move. Some will try to get to the West, but millions, especially the poorest, will head for India and run up against the fence and the border guards. India will then have an even greater humanitarian and political problem on its hands than now.

Muslims make up about 15 percent of Indians, or some 200 million. But in Bangladesh about 90 percent of people are Muslim. A crisis of mass migration would throw up a number of questions. Given the existing tensions with illegal immigrants, how many Bangladeshis would India take? How many would the majority population accept, especially in the border states, without riots breaking out and political parties rushing to extremes? Would India give preference to the Bangladeshi Hindus on the grounds that they suffer the most, given the levels of religious discrimination they claim to endure? Both countries already struggle with these issues, but the worst-case scenarios of flooding would greatly exacerbate them: climate change and economic hardship cause further movements of displaced people, who are not easily integrated culturally and economically into other nations.

Bangladesh has its own difficulties with displaced people. The Rohingya are a minority group of Muslims in the majority-Buddhist state of Myanmar. About 750,000 Rohingya live in the region of Arakan, which borders Bangladesh. They are ethnically related to the Chittagonians of southern Bangladesh, and they have a problem. The Rohingya are stateless, having been denied citizenship on the basis of ethnicity. In 1982 the Myanmar dictatorship drew up a citizenship law listing the 135 national "races" it claims were settled in the country prior to the beginning of British colonization of the Arakan region in 1823. Despite evidence that the Rohingya were present in the area as long ago as the seventh century, the junta classified them as not being from Myanmar. The Rohingya endure severe travel restrictions, find it difficult to get into business, and face an often fruitless struggle to register the births and marriages in their communities, thus being further isolated.

In the early 1990s up to 250,000 Rohingya fled to Bangladesh amid reports of religious persecution, murder, rape, torture, and forced labor by the Myanmar military. The UN High Commissioner for Refugees (UNHCR) regarded them as refugees, and at first Bangladesh accommodated them. But, faced with ever-increasing numbers, it started to forcibly deport tens of thousands back across the border, often amid clashes between the refugees and the Bangladeshi military. By the middle of the decade all but about twenty thousand were back in Myanmar. However, it is impossible to know for certain how many there are, as the Bangladeshi government stopped registering them and subsequently asked aid agencies to desist from helping the unregistered—so as to discourage others from coming. Despite being one of the poorest countries in the world, Bangladesh has taken in up to half a million refugees this century, but is woefully ill equipped to deal with them.

In 1998 the UNHCR wrote to the military government in Myanmar demanding equal treatment for the Rohingya following allegations of widespread discrimination and ill treatment. The junta wrote back, "They are racially, ethnically, culturally different from the other national races in our country. Their language as well as religion is also different." In recent years anti-Rohingya violence has increased again, with villages and mosques set on fire and people murdered, particularly in response to an attack on border police by a Rohingya militant group in August 2017. The number of people trying to get into Bangladesh has consequently risen dramatically again: over six hundred thousand were on the move in the second half of 2017 alone.

Hundreds of thousands of Rohingya are now living in shanty-towns around the Bangladeshi port town of Cox's Bazar or in UNHCR camps. In a poor, overcrowded country that struggles to take care of its own citizens, humanitarian resources are spread thinly, and these immigrants are often feared as a source of lawlessness and crime, being outside of society with no legal way of working. Some in Bangladesh have demanded tighter border controls in the wake of the latest influx of refugees; however, some have also called for a stronger humanitarian response. Unrest in the region could attract terrorist organizations, which would take advantage of the conflict, playing on the religious and ethnic divisions and spreading extremist ideas among the affected minority groups. The region could become a hotbed for radicalization, further inflaming the violence that has erupted there.

Bangladesh is set on returning the refugees as soon as possible; Myanmar has tended to prevaricate, suggesting that the refugees will be taken back, while planning to upgrade and expand the barrier along its 170-mile border with Bangladesh. Land mines have allegedly been laid to prevent people from returning. Furthermore, what could the Rohingya expect to return to? More than two hundred villages have been burned to the ground, and systematic discrimination against them still exists.

No obvious solution is in sight as long as Myanmar continues to hound its minorities; another border, therefore, looks set to remain a source of tension and instability.

The surging populations of the subcontinent are facing the challenges of the twenty-first century in a man-made geography of fences and national borders that has little respect for history.

To the south of Assam, the Rakhine Mountains separate India from Myanmar and are covered in dense jungle. People have made their way through the jungle to try to claim asylum in India, but not in such great numbers as to make it a national issue. Of more concern is the insurgency being fought by the tribal Naga people within Myanmar, which sometimes spills over into India and has led to the construction of a fence, not by the Indians but by Myanmar, along parts of that section of the border.

The Nagas are a collection of forested-hill tribes. They have cultural traditions in common, although their language is varied—most speak different dialects of the Naga root language that are unintelligible to outsiders and sometimes even to one another. Some tribes only gave up head-hunting a few decades ago after converting to Christianity, but they remain tied to many original cultural practices and do not see themselves as being from either Myanmar or India.

Following the declaration of the state of India in 1947 and the state of Myanmar the following year, the Naga people found themselves divided by the newly declared sovereign borders. An armed struggle broke out in the 1950s when some Naga tribesmen on the Indian side of the border began to agitate for independence from New Delhi. The creation of the state of Nagaland (India's smallest) in 1963 reduced the level of violence but did not result in a permanent settlement. By the 1970s the militants had been driven into Myanmar, but continued their struggle from there alongside other Naga tribes. An estimated 2 million Nagas are now spread across both sides of the frontier, an area that Naga nationalists want to turn into a united homeland.

The Myanmar government, which is at any time usually dealing with several internal insurgencies, did little to prevent the Nagas from using the region to train and equip their militias and conduct frequent cross-border raids. This has been a major source of irritation to the national government in India and the state governments in Assam, Manipur, and Nagaland. In 2015, following a raid that killed eighteen Indian soldiers, the Indian military conducted a lightning nighttime cross-border operation, the first in many years. Helicopters dropped Indian commandos at the border, who pushed several miles into Myanmar before attacking two Naga rebel camps. New Delhi claimed that around thirty-eight rebels were killed, although that figure is disputed.

Publicly the Myanmar government had to pretend to be angry about the incursion, but it had occasionally crossed into the Indian states of Manipur and Mizoram in hot pursuit of "terrorists" from the Chin and Arakanese rebel groups and so in private tolerated the incursion into its sovereign territory. Undiplomatically, the Indian government trumpeted the whole affair, causing Myanmar to think hard about how to prevent further such actions. An added impetus was China's increasing influence in Myanmar, which could be counterbalanced by forging stronger ties with India.

In early 2017, with Indian army operations continuing against the insurgents, Myanmar began to construct a short border fence in the Naga Self-Administered Zone, a region where the Naga people enjoy limited autonomy. Officially, India is not involved with the fence; however, New Delhi does give Myanmar $5 million a year to promote "border areas development" in the region. The fence is there in the name of mutual national security, both to prevent the Naga militia from entering India and to ensure that no one from India constructs any buildings on Myanmar's side of the frontier. The Myanmar government says its purpose is not to restrict the movement of ordinary people, but the fence does nevertheless threaten to split up communities and families, who until now treated the nation-state borders as imaginary. The two governments had acquiesced in this with the Free Movement Regime, which allowed the Nagas to travel up to ten miles on either side of the border without requiring visas. This helped to grow border markets, where the Myanmar Nagas could buy Indian products mostly unavailable at home and which had previously been smuggled across the border. All of this is now under threat and will further divide a people who regard themselves as neither Indian nor Burmese, but as Naga.

Not all of India's borders are so troubled that they've been fenced off. India and Bhutan have a close relationship, and because India accounts for 98 percent of Bhutan's exports, neither side is contemplating "hardening" the border. Although India's relations with Nepal are more strained, especially after a four-month "blockade" of the border in 2015, New Delhi does not see the need to fence what is a thousand-mile frontier, especially as it is keen to maintain influence in the country and not permit a vacuum it knows the Chinese would fill.

A natural barrier—the Himalayas—separates China and India along much of their twenty-five-hundred-mile-long frontier, so they are pretty much walled off from each other. The Indian state of Arunachal Pradesh is claimed by China, but the dispute has not resulted in a hostile border, although 2017 saw a nonviolent standoff in the Himalayan Doklam Plateau after India accused

China of building roads. New Delhi fears this could allow China to move armored columns across the plateau and down into India. If so, China could cut what is known as the "chicken's neck," a relatively narrow corridor of land that would then divide the bulk of India from its northeastern states.

Where we start to hit real trouble again is along the Indian border with Pakistan. Since partition, relations between the two countries have been fraught, and this is very much a "hot" border. India has built a 340-mile-long barrier along the disputed Line of Control (cease-fire line) inside Kashmir, a region both countries say is their sovereign territory. Most of it is 150 yards inside the Indian-controlled side and consists of double-row fencing up to twelve feet high. It is similar to the West Bengal–Bangladesh fence, with motion sensors and thermal-imaging technology linked to a command system to warn rapid-response border troops of any incursions. The strip of land between the two fences is mined.

In 1947, under the Indian Independence Act, states were given the choice of joining India or Pakistan or becoming independent. Maharaja Hari Singh, the ruler of Kashmir, was Hindu, whereas most of his people were Muslim. The maharaja chose neutrality, sparking a Pakistan-encouraged Muslim uprising, which in turn led the maharaja to cede Kashmir to India. That sparked a full-scale war; as a result the territory was divided, but on both sides the majority of the population is Muslim. Another war followed in 1965, and serious clashes occurred in 1999 between Indian forces and Pakistani-sponsored groups. By this time both nations were nuclear armed, and the prevention of conflict between them became even more important. A low-level insurgency continues on the Indian-controlled side of Kashmir, and this, the bitterest dispute between the two powers, sporadically threatens to worsen. Talks come and go, gestures of friendship are made, often through cricket matches, but India has concluded that until the issues are resolved, one way to keep the peace is to build barriers to prevent infiltrations by insurgent groups that could spark full-scale fighting.

This vast project has taken decades, but New Delhi is now filling in the gaps in its northern and western border defenses, having already fenced parts of the Punjab and Rajasthan in the 1980s and 1990s, and is working to "seal" its entire western border, from Gujurat on the Arabian Sea right up to Kashmir in the Himalayas, with what it calls a Comprehensive Integrated Border Management System (CIBMS). Some of this terrain is already difficult to cross due to swampland in the south, and to the north the Thar Desert.

The CIBMS is a similar system to that on the Bangladesh frontier, but this is a much more active border, and the danger of military action between India and Pakistan is ever present. The new barriers going up all have radar, thermal imaging, night vision, and other equipment linked to control rooms that appear every three miles. Two hundred thousand floodlights are planned, and the 130 sectors that are riverine will have underwater lasers linked to the control centers. The Indian military is also looking at buying unmanned aerial vehicles (UAVs) capable of identifying a newspaper from sixty thousand feet, as well as equipment that can detect human movement tens of miles away. Pakistan has criticized the building of the barriers, saying they violate UN resolutions and local agreements; but India says that incidents of cross-border shelling and militia raids are being lessened by its measures.

Issues such as this are open to interpretation. While India might see the construction of a fortified lookout post as defensive, Pakistan could regard it as a launchpad for an offensive. The India Pakistan Border Ground Rules Agreement (1960–61) sets out how to accommodate both points of view, but it has never been signed by either side, and in practice such agreements are arrived at ad hoc. Each year can throw up a matter of contention that had not necessarily been clarified in the early 1960s. For example, in 2017 India erected a 360-foot-high flagpole at the Attari border in Punjab. Pakistan immediately accused India of violating the agreement, saying that the flagpole, which could be seen from the city of Lahore, might have been fitted with cameras to allow India to spy on Pakistan.

The situation in Kashmir is more formal. Even without an agreement on where the border should be, in theory behavior on each side of the Line of Control (LoC) is regulated by the Karachi Agreement of 1949. It says that no defenses should be constructed within five hundred yards of each side of the line, a stipulation frequently ignored by both sides. The fragile cease-fire is also frequently broken. Not only do cross-border shootings occur between Indian and Pakistani regular forces, but New Delhi accuses Islamabad of sponsoring terrorist groups to cross into the Indian-controlled side to foment violence and even carry out attacks in Indian cities. Since the early 1980s the two countries have engaged in sporadic artillery duels high up on the Siachen Glacier close to the LoC. Located on the Karakoram Range in the Himalayas, this is the world's highest combat zone. At almost twenty thousand feet above sea level Pakistani and Indian soldiers face off in one of the most hostile climates possible. Tours of duty at the higher levels are only twelve weeks long as lack of oxygen can prevent sleep and cause hallucinations. The soldiers exchange fire, but frostbite causes more casualties than high explosives.

Kashmir remains the biggest issue between the two countries. They share a border drawn by outsiders; it divided communities and now stands as a fortified monument to the enmity between two nuclear-armed nations.

Pakistan's 1,510-mile-long western border with Afghanistan was also shaped by outsiders. The original Muslim conquerors used Afghanistan as a jumping-off point from which to invade India, and the British then used it to delineate the western periphery of the jewel in the crown of their empire. The border is still known as the Durand Line, after Sir Henry Mortimer Durand. In 1893 he and the Afghan emir Abdur Rahman Khan drew the line that effectively established Afghanistan as a buffer zone between British-controlled India and Russian-controlled Central Asia.

It was, is, and will remain a problematic frontier. It separates Pashtuns on each side of it into citizens of different countries, a separation many do not accept. For that reason, and because Afghanistan claims some territory east of the line, Kabul does not recognize the border.

Pakistan, desperate to prevent Pashtun nationalism leading to secession, prefers a weak Afghanistan. This, in part, is why sections of the Pakistani military establishment covertly support the Taliban and other groups inside Afghanistan—even though this has come back to bite them east of the Durand Line. There are now the Afghan Taliban and the Pakistan Taliban, which have close ties and similar views, and both of which kill Pakistani civilians and military personnel.

By the spring of 2017 things had become so bad that Pakistan announced plans to build a fence in two districts along the border in the Federally Administered Tribal Areas. This, it was said, was to combat cross-border operations by the Taliban. However, even if the Pakistanis manage to construct fencing in this difficult and mountainous terrain, the genie is out of the bottle: the Taliban are inside the country and able to move around.

Meanwhile, to the south of the Durand Line is the Pakistan-Iran border, and here it is the Iranians who are building a wall. A ten-foot-high, three-foot-thick concrete wall is rising along parts of the frontier. This follows years of drug smuggling, but also the infiltration of Sunni militia groups from Pakistan into Iran, which is a majority-Shia country. In 2014 Iranian troops crossed the border to take on a militant group; they then had a firefight with Pakistani border guards. Relations remain cordial between the two states, but in the age of walls Iran is attempting physical separation to prevent the situation from deteriorating, thus continuing the trend set by India, Bangladesh, and other nations in the region.

All of the above examples fly in the face of the dream of some politicians, and many people in the business community, of creating a vast open trading zone in the subcontinent. India in particular has been reaching out to Myanmar, Nepal, Bhutan, and Bangladesh to develop plans for easier travel and trade across the region. Transnational road and rail links are envisaged, with streamlined crossing points and even, eventually, a huge reduction in border controls similar to the ones in parts of the EU. Progress, however, is slow, and the border-building programs now seen in most of the countries go against the practicalities and spirit of regional cooperation.

We see the deepest divide on the India-Pakistan and the India-Bangladesh borders because this is, at heart, a religious one. India is a Hindu-majority country with a secular democratic system and traditions, but in recent years it has seen a sharp growth in Hindu nationalism. Pakistan is an Islamic republic with a troubled democracy and a history of military rule, while Bangladesh, although nominally a secular republic, has become increasingly religious in both the state sector and public life, with minorities and atheists at serious risk of being murdered for their beliefs.

Not all the walls in the subcontinent are made of stone or wire; some are invisible, but they are present all the same. India has massive internal divisions on a scale and level of prejudice that would, if repeated in some countries, be regarded as a shocking scandal requiring international condemnation—yet the world is mostly silent about the horrors of the Indian caste system.

The system has echoes of apartheid, albeit with significant differences—not least being that it is not enshrined in the country's laws. Nevertheless, it has created a segregated society within which some humans are classified as superior beings and others as impure, and people must remain "in their place." Certain categories of people are denied entry to jobs and have their movements restricted. The system ensures that a ruling caste maintains positions of privilege and condemns others to a life of poverty in which they are subject to violence without recourse to legal redress. The walls between the castes are mostly invisible to outsiders.

The roots of the caste system are religious and date back more than three thousand years. Hindus are divided into rigid hierarchical groups based on what they do for a living. This is justified in the *Manusmriti*, the most authoritative book on Hindu law, which regards the system as the "basis of order and regularity of society." Higher castes live among each other, eating and drinking places are segregated, intermarriage is usually banned or at least frowned upon, and in practice many jobs are closed to lower castes.

Some preindustrial European societies were based on the hereditary transmission of occupation, which ensured the class system remained intact, but it wasn't based on religion and has been massively weakened by modernity. The Indian caste system is also fraying in some places due to the pressures of urban living, but its religious basis ensures that it is embedded in everyday life. India remains a predominantly rural society, and thus the ability to hide your roots and avoid your religious heritage is limited. However, even as the population slowly shifts to the cities, the caste system endures because the religious system does.

The system has four main categories of people: Brahmans, Kshatriyas, Vaishyas, and Sudras. Brahma is the god of creation, and the Brahmans, who dominate education and the intellectual fields, are said to have come from his head. The Kshatriyas (from Brahma's arms) are warriors and rulers, while the Vaishyas (from his thighs) are traders, and the Sudras (from his feet) do the menial work. These four categories are split among about three thousand castes, which are in turn divided into twenty-five thousand subcastes.

Outside of the system are the untouchables, now mostly called the Dalits, "broken people." In India, if you see someone disposing of a dead animal or sweeping the streets, chances are the person is a Dalit. Anyone cleaning toilets or working in sewers is almost certainly a Dalit. They are much more likely to be victims of crime, especially rape, murder, and beatings, although conviction rates for people charged with crimes against Dalits are significantly lower than for crimes committed against other groups. In many rural areas Dalits are still not allowed to draw water from public wells or enter Hindu temples. The caste you are born into dictates the job you will have, and lower-caste people will find themselves with a broom in their hands even if they have a university education. All of the lower castes suffer from discrimination, but at the very bottom are the Dalits.

The caste system has an element of skin color that many people like to downplay, but it is there nonetheless. A 2016 genetic study by Hyderabad's Centre for Cellular & Molecular Biology discovered a "profound influence on skin pigmentation patterns" within the class structure, the lighter skin tones being predominantly found among the higher castes. National secular laws have in theory banned discrimination, but as the system is dominated by people in the higher castes who want to maintain it, the laws are not enforced. Many politicians are also reluctant to take real action as they rely on bloc votes from certain castes.

The system is deeply embedded in the culture of the country. For example, Mahatma Gandhi, who was from one of the higher castes, said, "I believe that if Hindu society has been able to stand, it is because it is founded on the caste system. . . . To destroy the caste system and adopt the Western European social system means that Hindus must give up the principle of hereditary occupation, which is the soul of the caste system. Hereditary principle is an eternal principle. To change it is to create disorder." To be fair to Gandhi, he did later speak out against the caste system and the treatment of the untouchables. However, he continued to defend the idea of *varnas*, or social classes. He said everyone was assigned a hereditary calling that defined what job he or she should do, but that this did not imply levels of superiority. *Varnas*, he wrote, were "the law of life universally governing the human family."

This sense of entitlement and "natural law" remains endemic. The Dalits, and other castes, have been using the secular laws to try to level the playing field. They have had some success, but it has also led to rising levels of violence against them. India's 2014 National Crime Records showed a 29 percent increase in crime against lower-caste people over two years as they increasingly resort to the law to seek justice. Dalits owning or buying land is the most common cause of violence against them by local communities determined to keep them at the bottom of society.

Reliable national statistics for caste numbers are difficult to find because the last time the Indian census included caste was 1931. Then the untouchables constituted 12.5 percent of the population. Now, despite twenty-seven years of affirmative action, they remain the poorest and most oppressed of India's people. The major government, judicial, diplomatic, and military positions, as well as senior posts in major companies, academia, the media, and the education system, are all overwhelmingly dominated by Brahmans despite the fact that they compose roughly 3.5 percent of the population. All societies build in social stratification, but even the elite public school system in Britain's class-based society does not result in such a rigid, ossified social structure. Given the rural and religious base of Indian culture, it will take a long time for these prejudices to be overcome—should enough Indians even want to. The system survives partially because its supporters openly argue that it binds society together: India needs to be protected from the fragmentation of society witnessed in Europe after the Industrial Revolution. Its opponents counter that it is immoral and holds the country back as it cannot harness all of its human talents.

Over the decades since independence some Dalits have surmounted the obstacles and risen to prominence, notably K. R. Narayanan, who served as president between 1997 and 2002. With people increasingly moving from the countryside to the cities, the invisible walls are beginning to grow weaker: what caste you are is less obvious in the city, some urbanites do not take the system so seriously, and even some caste intermarriages are now occurring. But P. L. Mimroth of the Centre for Dalit Rights believes that the roots of discrimination are still so deeply embedded in the national psyche that it will take generations until the spirit of the laws against the caste system is truly accepted: "We were wrong to believe that education would eradicate untouchability. It will take more than one hundred years to change that."

As the statistics show, the system is still alive and well throughout the country: tens of millions of people are denied basic human rights, not by law but by culture. This is not the image of India most people have. Generations of tourists and student backpackers return from India infused with the spirit of Hinduism, which promotes friendliness, nonviolence, spiritualism, and vegetarianism. Few see that alongside that is one of the most degrading social systems on the planet.

In 1936 the great Indian intellectual B. R. Ambedkar was invited to deliver the annual lecture to a Hindu reformist group. He submitted his speech, which included, among many other challenging statements, "There cannot be a more degrading system of social organization than the caste system. . . . It is the system that deadens, paralyses and cripples the people from helpful activity." The lecture was canceled on the grounds that parts of it were "unbearable." Ambedkar published his work as an essay later that year.

In the twenty-first century Indian society is far from "dead-ened"—indeed India is a vibrant, increasingly important country, embracing a range of high-tech industries—yet within it are millions of barriers to progress for tens of millions of its citizens. The walls around India are designed to keep people out, and those within to keep people down.

The divides throughout the subcontinent are becoming ever more apparent, exacerbated by the continuing and growing movement of people escaping poverty, persecution, and climate change. If the majority of scientists are correct in their predictions of climate change, then it is obvious people will continue to be on the move this century. A wall has yet to be built that can withstand that much weight pressing against it. The barriers can and will be built as a partial, one-sided, temporary holding "solution," but unless prosperity is also built, everyone is going to lose. In an attempt to control the regional demographics, the barriers along the majority of the thousands of miles of frontiers are now being built higher and wider and are becoming more technologically sophisticated. As we've seen, though, such barriers don't stop people from attempting to cross anyway—many don't have any other choice but to try—and increasingly violent policing of borders can lead to terrible human consequences. Felani Khatun paid with her life, and down in the delta plains of Bangladesh are millions more like her.

CHAPTER 6

Africa

The forces that unite us are intrinsic and greater than the superimposed influences that keep us apart.

—Kwame Nkrumah

Previous pages: A Sahrawi girl with Sahrawi flag in front of the Moroccan Wall, separating Western Sahara between territory controlled by Morocco and that held by the Polisario Front.

At the top of Africa is a wall of sand, of shame, and of silence. The Moroccan Wall runs for seventeen hundred miles through Western Sahara and into parts of Morocco. The whole construction separates what Morocco terms its Southern Provinces along the Atlantic coast from the Free Zone in the desert interior—an area the Sahrawi people call the Sahrawi Arab Democratic Republic. The barrier is built of sand piled almost seven feet high, with a backing trench and millions of land mines stretching several miles into the desert on each side. It is thought to be the longest continuous minefield in the world. Every three miles or so is a Moroccan army outpost with up to forty troops, some of whom patrol the spaces between the bases, while two and a half miles back from each major post are rapid-reaction mobile units, and behind those, artillery bases. The length of the wall is also dotted with radar masts that can "see" up to fifty miles into the Free Zone. All of this is intended to keep fighters from the Sahrawi military force, called the Polisario Front (PF), well away from the wall and the areas Morocco considers its territory.

It is a harsh place. By day the heat can reach 122°F, and at night the temperature can drop to almost freezing. Frequently the sand-laden sirocco wind blows through the arid land, turning the air a mustard color and restricting visibility. To an outsider it is a hostile, forbidding region, but to the Sahrawi people, it's home.

A Western Saharan independence movement existed prior to Spain's withdrawal from the region in 1975. As the Spanish left, 350,000 Moroccans took part in the "Green March"—they

walked into the region and claimed it as Moroccan territory. Spain
subsequently transferred control to Morocco and Mauritania; the
government in Rabat effectively annexed the territory and sent in
twenty thousand troops, who were immediately confronted by the
PF. The fighting lasted sixteen years and took the lives of tens of
thousands of people. Despite their superior numbers and modern
military equipment, the Moroccan army could not subdue the
PF and their guerrilla tactics. In 1980, Morocco began building
what became known as the Wall of Shame, finishing it in 1987.

Now there is silence. Western Sahara is not so much a forgotten
conflict as a conflict few people have ever heard of. The Sahrawi
people who live on each side of the wall speak the Hassaniya
dialect of Arabic, feel culturally different from Moroccans, and
are traditionally a nomadic people, although now they are mostly
urban and tens of thousands live in refugee camps. Moroccan
immigration has completely changed the composition of the
Western Saharan population as the government has encouraged
people to settle there by offering tax breaks, subsidies, and one-
off payments. The total population of the remaining Sahrawi is
not known, but estimates range between two hundred thousand
and four hundred thousand. Until the mid-twentieth century
they'd had no concept of borders; they simply moved over a vast
area, following unpredictable rainfall. Now, 85 percent of what
they would regard as their traditional territory is under Moroccan
control. The word *Sahrawi* means "inhabitants of the desert,"
and that is what they wish to be—not inhabitants of Morocco.
They are, like other peoples we will encounter throughout this
chapter, victims of the lines drawn by others—in this case a vast
line made of, and in, the sand.

Morocco is not alone in dealing with secessionist movements.
Across Africa attempts are being made to break away, conflicts
that descend into incredibly violent civil wars, such as those we've
seen in South Sudan and the Democratic Republic of the Congo.

Why do so many African countries suffer such terrible strife? The reasons are many and varied, but the history of the way in which the nation-states across the continent were formed plays a crucial part.

Independence movements struggle for recognition and self-determination. The idea of the nation-state, having developed in Europe, spread like wildfire in the nineteenth and twentieth centuries, calling for self-determining government for a "nation" of people—a group who to some degree share a historical, ethnic, cultural, geographical, or linguistic community.

When the European colonialists drew their lines on maps and created the nation-states that, largely, still make up the continent of Africa, they were treating a vast landmass containing a rich diversity of peoples, customs, cultures, and ethnicities with little regard for any of them—and the nation-states they created often bore no relation at all to the nations that were already there. These nations—or peoples—are sometimes referred to as tribes. Western writers are often squeamish about using the word *tribe*, and some Western and African academics will even tell you the colonialists invented the concept. They are simply playing with words because they are embarrassed that the word *tribe* has, wrongly, for some people become synonymous with "backwardness." Nevertheless, tribes exist within many nation-states in Africa and elsewhere—it seems pointless to deny their importance.

I have a friend in London who is from West Africa. The first thing he told me about himself was his name, then that he was from Ivory Coast, and then that he was from the Mandinka tribe. This was to him a source of pride, an identification with a people spread across several West African countries in each of which they compose a significant minority. He is not unusual: huge numbers of Africans use the word *tribe* to refer to their nation or people and identify with whichever one they belong to. Within this there will be, to varying degrees, a shared history, customs, food, and possibly language and religion. In this the Africans are no different from any other peoples around the world; what does distinguish them is how strong this tribalism remains within many African nation-states. An English family abroad, meeting another, may well share a strained conversation along the lines of "Ah, a Brit. Where are you from?" "Milton Keynes." "Oh, Milton Keynes," followed by short periods of silence broken possibly by a discussion about which are the best roads into Milton Keynes. A Mandinka from Ivory Coast meeting another from Gambia when visiting Nigeria will have a lot more to talk about.

Classifications are difficult, but Africa is estimated to have at least three thousand ethnic groups encompassing a huge variety of languages, religions, and cultures. Among the largest are the Amhara and Oromo in Ethiopia, which comprise about 54 million people. Nigeria is home to four of the ten largest tribes on the continent—the Yoruba, Hausa, Igbo, and Ijaw, totaling almost 100 million in a country of 186 million people. The Shona in Zimbabwe, the Zulu in South Africa, and the Ashanti in Ghana each number about 10 million. Many smaller groups and subgroups exist, however. As a rough guide, and depending on how they are counted, Nigeria alone is estimated to have between 250 and 500 tribes.

Tribalism can have many positive aspects, providing a sense of community, a shared history, values and customs, and a source of support in troubled times. Even with increasing urbanization, these tribal traditions have continued and created new communities as people group together.

Usually, as a newcomer to a city, you will head to a district where you feel socially accepted and where people will show you the ropes. Frequently that will be among folk who you identify with, which gives you the feeling of safety in numbers—this quickly leads to the re-creation of a tribe. We witness this everywhere, in every Chinatown in the world, for example, and we see it in

African cities such as Nairobi in Kenya, where often people from different tribes around the country settle in districts of the city populated by those of the same tribe. A Luhya from a rural area of Kenya who moves to the capital might more quickly feel at home in the Kawangware district, even if it is one of the poorer parts of town. The Kenyan tribes have carved out extended tribal villages within Nairobi. This has been going on for decades across the continent. In the 1986 novel *Coming to Birth* by the Kenyan writer Marjorie Oludhe Macgoye, the main character, a sixteen-year-old girl named Paulina who is from the Luo tribe, arrives in Nairobi from rural Kisumu and heads for the Makongeni district. Makongeni was, and remains, mostly populated by Luo.

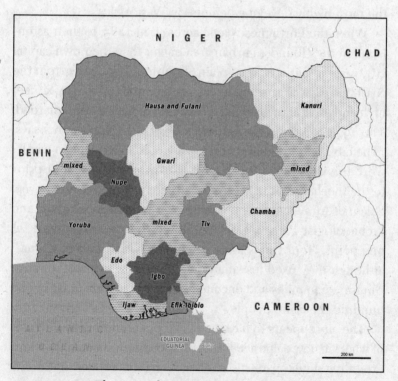

The various linguistic regions of Nigeria.

While belonging to a tribe is a positive thing, a source of pride for many, in Africa—as elsewhere—one key question is the degree to which the existence of tribes holds back the forging of the biggest tribal unit, the nation-state, and the cohesion it is supposed to represent. The problem lies in the way in which the nation-states were formed.

Drive several hours east of Lagos and you can find, with some difficulty, the ruins of a massive walled city that was lost to the jungle, and then to history, for centuries. The walls are thought to have been begun in the eighth century to repel invaders. By the eleventh century Benin City was the capital of the Benin Empire, the most highly developed empire in West Africa.

When the Portuguese came across it in 1485, to their astonishment they found an urban area bigger than their own capital city, Lisbon. Situated on a plain about four days' walk from the coast, the city was surrounded by massive walls up to sixty-six feet high and exceptionally deep ditches, all of which were guarded. The 1974 edition of the *Guinness Book of World Records* says, "The city walls, together with those in the kingdom as a whole, were the world's second-largest earthworks carried out prior to the mechanical era." A 1990s article by Fred Pearce in *New Scientist* (drawing on the work of the British geographer and archaeologist Patrick Darling) stated that the walls were, at one point, "four times longer than the Great Wall of China," although they used less material. They are estimated to have run for 9,940 miles and encompassed a population of up to one hundred thousand people.

The city appears to have been laid out according to the rules of what we now call fractal design—a complex repeating pattern exhibiting similar patterns at increasingly small scales. In the city center was the palace of the king, who oversaw a highly bureaucratic society. From this fanned out thirty main streets, about 120 feet wide, running at right angles to one another, all with narrower streets leading off them. The city was split into eleven neighborhoods. Some were lit at night by tall metal lamps with palm-oil-fueled wicks that illuminated the extensive artwork to be found across the city. Inside the city were houses, some two stories high, and walled compounds made of red clay. Outside were five hundred walled villages, all connected to one another and to the capital. A moat system included twenty smaller moats around some villages and towns.

The early Portuguese explorers were impressed with the scale of the city and the stunning works of art and architecture it contained. In 1691 Lourenco Pinto, a Portuguese ship's captain, observed, "All the streets run straight and as far as the eye can see. The houses are large, especially that of the king, which is richly decorated and has fine columns. The city is wealthy and industrious. It is so well governed that theft is unknown and the people live in such security that they have no doors to their houses."

In 1897 this jewel of West Africa was destroyed by British troops as they tried to expand their control of the continent. After a few years of British attempts to consolidate their power over the region, the situation had descended into violence. A force of twelve hundred or so Royal Marines fell upon the city, burning the palace and people's homes and looting religious icons and works of art. Many of the stolen Benin bronzes remain in museums around the world even today. The king escaped but later returned and was exiled to southern Nigeria, where he died in 1914.

By then most of the great city walls had been destroyed as the victorious British stamped their authority on the kingdom, blowing up large sections of the walls and incorporating the city and its surroundings into "British Nigeria." Local people took much of what was left as building materials to make new homes, and slowly the city was depopulated. What remained was mostly forgotten about, except by people in the region. In the early 1960s archaeologists began to explore the area and map what is now a UNESCO World Heritage Site, as are the remains of a similar complex of walls and ditches in what is called Sungbo's Eredo, 140 miles to the west.

Although barely anything is left to indicate that Benin City even existed, it was a prime example of the richness, diversity, and wealth of precolonial African civilizations. When these kingdoms rose to power, they were separate entities; now they are but small parts of a much larger whole—Nigeria. The Europeans' border lines, such as those of "British Nigeria," were often drawn according to how far European explorers had gone, rather than taking into account the existing nations and kingdoms, which had organically evolved around tribal divisions. The Europeans forcibly threw together hundreds of nations, or tribes.

The myriad African nations were never democracies, but a ruler was usually from the same wider tribe as his subjects in a system of government originating from within that tribe. When the colonialists withdrew, different peoples were told they were now grouped together in a defined area, and they were often left with a ruler who, in the eyes of many, did not have the right to rule them. The colonial legacy has a double contradiction: first, the creation of single nation-states out of multiple nations and tribes; second, the Europeans simultaneously bequeathed ideas of democracy and self-determination. Much of the current discord and conflict we see in Africa is rooted in this experiment in rapid unification.

The first generation of leaders of the independent African states understood that any attempt to redraw the colonial maps might lead to hundreds of mini wars, so they decided to work with the existing lines in the hope of building genuine nation-states and thus reducing ethnic divisions. However, most leaders then failed to implement policies to unite their peoples within these borders, instead relying on brute force and repeating the colonialists' trick of divide and rule. The many different peoples thrown together in these newly minted nation-states had not had the beneficial experience of settling their differences and coming together over centuries. Some states are still struggling with the contradictions built into their systems by colonialism.

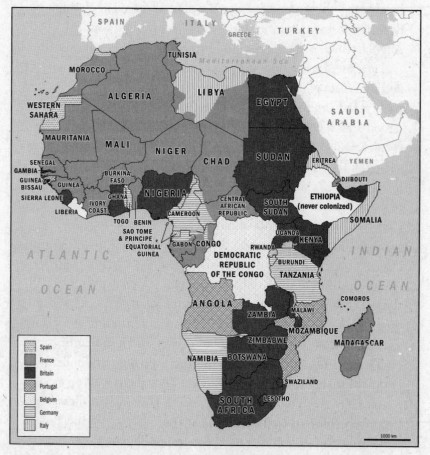

The territories occupied by colonial powers in Africa.

Angola is a prime example. It is larger than the US states of Oklahoma, Arkansas, Kansas, and Mississippi combined. When the Portuguese arrived in the sixteenth century the region was home to at least ten major ethnic groups subdivided into perhaps one hundred tribes. The Portuguese would have gone farther and incorporated even more nations into their colony, but they bumped up against British, Belgian, and German claims. The different ethnic groups had little in common—other than a dislike of their colonial masters. By the early 1960s enough of them had banded together to launch a war of independence. The Portuguese departed in 1975, but they left behind an invented country called Angola, which was expected to function as a united nation-state.

Imagine for a moment that colonialism had not happened, and that instead, as it modernized, Africa had followed a similar pattern to Europe and developed its own relatively homogeneous nation-states. One of the peoples of Angola are the Bakongo, who speak Kikongo, a Bantu language, and who in precolonial days had a kingdom of contiguous territory, stretching across parts of several territories including what are now Angola, DRC, and Gabon. They feel kinship with fellow Kikongo speakers in the Republic of the Congo and the Democratic Republic of the Congo—together comprising around 10 million people. In the DRC they are the largest ethnic group, but in Angola they are a minority, which explains the rise of the Bundu dia Kongo movement, which is present in all three countries and wants a nation-state of Kikongo speakers based on precolonial ideas of territory. They are still working at forging a unified nation-state—as are many others with a similar history.

There is no getting away from the aspiring nationalism of peoples torn apart by the colonial era. They did not agree to join federations given names by Europeans. Then, when they were eventually able to throw the Europeans out, they were expected to feel loyalty to a system that had been imposed upon them against their will, and in which too often the main ethnic group dominated all the others. In some countries these divisions can be contained within the political sphere, but in many places the lid has blown off, bringing civil war and the rise of separatist movements.

Take, for example, the Land and Maritime Boundary dispute between Cameroon and Nigeria, which began in 1994. Both countries claimed sovereignty over an oil-rich peninsula named Bakassi. The situation deteriorated so badly it led to sporadic armed conflict between them, leading to the emergence of the Bakassi Self-Determination Front (BSDF), which issues videos of members wearing uniforms and clutching assault rifles and runs a pirate radio station called Dayspring, which calls for self-rule. Cameroon has other problems with independence-minded people. It is a mainly French-speaking country, but out of a population of 23 million, a minority of about 5 million speak English. Some of the latter claim to be discriminated against, with growing calls for autonomy for the two western provinces bordering Nigeria in which most of them live. There's even a "president" in exile, a flag, and a national anthem ready in the unlikely event that the two provinces unite as Southern Cameroon.

There are many other examples. Casamance, a region in the southern part of Senegal, has been fighting for autonomy. Kenya has the Mombasa Republican Council, which wants independence for the country's coastal region, arguing that it has its own distinct culture and should not have been included as part of Kenya when it won independence from the UK. Its slogan, in Kiswahili, is *Pwani si Kenya*—"the coast is not Kenya." The Kenyans also have a problem with terrorism coming from Somalia, and so authorities spent much of 2018 building a partially electrified fence along the entirety of their shared border.

Few of the numerous secessionist movements are likely to be successful in the near to medium future, but breakaways cannot be ruled out—some have managed it in recent years. Ethiopia lost Eritrea to an independence movement and still faces separatist factions in its Ogaden and Oromia regions, while Sudan is split into two countries, South Sudan having become the world's newest state in 2011. Sadly, the situation there has degenerated into civil war: the dominant Dinka tribe was quickly accused of discriminating against the Nuer, Acholi, and others, which led to fighting between them. The war has cost several hundred thousands lives and caused more than a million people to flee their homes.

It's a familiar story in the recent history of Africa. Perhaps one of the worst examples was in Nigeria, where a massacre of the Igbos preceded the civil war of 1967–70 and the short-lived Republic of Biafra; in total more than 3 million were killed, and Nigeria has a continuing problem with Biafran ideas of nationhood. But this is far from the only case. Burundi is another. Ethnically it is about 85 percent Hutu, but the 14 percent Tutsi minority are politically and economically powerful, and the country has long been ravaged by the tensions between them. In 1965 a coup attempt against the king, who was a Tutsi, sparked ethnic fighting that killed at least five thousand people. In 1972 mass killings sparked an invasion by Hutu rebels who had based themselves in Zaire. It is thought that over the following four years almost two hundred thousand people died. Smaller outbreaks of violence plagued the 1980s before a full-scale civil war broke out in 1993 and continued until 2005. This time Hutu president Melchior Ndadaye was killed by Tutsi assassins, setting off a chain of events that pitted the two sides against each other. The last few years have witnessed low-level violence, with about four hundred thousand Burundians fleeing the country, most heading for Tanzania.

In Rwanda around eight hundred thousand Tutsis and moderate Hutus were murdered in the 1994 genocide. The Democratic Republic of the Congo contains more than two hundred ethnic groups and has been suffering terrible violence since 1996—estimates vary, but some put the death toll as high as 6 million, and the agony of the conflict continues today. A whole host of other countries, including Liberia and Angola, have also endured widespread and sustained conflict. The factors behind the violence are complex and include the imposition of borders, a lack of development, and poverty; but without doubt the ethnic divides are significant. Since the nations still frequently cross nation-state borders, conflict in one can quickly spread to another.

All nation-states have differences with their neighbors, but in most other parts of the world territorial disputes arose organically over long periods and were based on geography and ethnicity. In many cases they have been settled. However, the African experience is of relatively recent geographical and ethnic contradictions being built into the whole region by outsiders. Yes, we're back to colonialism—because there will be no getting away from it until the Africans can distance themselves from its effects. Given the scale of the social engineering, sixty to seventy years of independence is no distance at all.

It does not help that the European borders are still the basis of any diplomatic resolution of territorial disputes—as we saw in Morocco and Western Sahara, which are still abiding by the lines drawn by Spain. Unsure of how to respond or with whom to side, the international community has recognized neither Morocco nor the Polisario Front's claim to Western Sahara; the region is on the United Nations list of Non-Self-Governing Territories, meaning that the area hasn't officially been decolonized. So technically Spain is still the administering power in Western Sahara, even though in practice most of it is under Moroccan control.

Another example is the dispute between Cameroon and Nigeria, which was eventually taken to the International Court of Justice (ICJ) and settled in 2002. Interestingly, both countries went to court citing not ancient tribal claims, nor the wishes of the present-day inhabitants, but colonial-era documents drawn up and signed by Europeans, when the British ruled Nigeria and Cameroon was part of the German Empire. These documents were the basis of the ICJ judgment stating that "sovereignty over the Bakassi Peninsula lies with Cameroon" and that "the boundary is delimited by the Anglo-German agreement of 11 March 1913." The court noted that the boundary dispute "falls within an historical framework including partition by European powers in the nineteenth and early twentieth centuries, League of Nations mandates, UN Trusteeships and the independence of the two states."

Not all Nigerians are happy with the ICJ ruling, nor with their then government's decision to abide by it. Some want the issue reopened. The *Vanguard* newspaper of the Niger Delta region has been campaigning for years to have the ruling reversed, and to revisit the case on the basis of ancestral land claims. One recent opinion piece ended, "To reclaim Bakassi Peninsula is a task that must be done!"

Academics argue about the extent to which the various disputes and conflicts are actually underpinned by ethnicity. Some suggest that politicians are just using the different factions to further their own aims. This may well sometimes be the case, but it does not mean that the differences are not there to be exploited, or that they do not run deep.

In some cases strong tribal affiliations can distract policy makers from focusing on what is in the national interest and can split politics along tribal lines. The relatively stable South African democracy, for example, is supposed to be ethnically blind, but the political system is splintered along ethnic and tribal lines: the Zulu are linked with the Inkatha Freedom Party, for instance, while the Xhosa dominate the ANC. The constitution of the country recognized these divides and set up Provincial Houses of Traditional Leaders in Limpopo, KwaZulu-Natal, Eastern Cape, Free State, Mpumalanga, and North West. They are in essence reflective of different South African "nations" or tribes.

Another political issue is that tribalism also encourages favoritism—or, to put it another way, corruption. This is a huge problem across the whole continent, described by Kenya's former president Daniel arap Moi as a "cancer," which impacts in all sorts of ways. Political appointments, business deals, and legal judgments can all be affected by it, which means the best person for the job is often not the person who gets it. It discourages marriage from outside a defined group, and it militates against national unity. It's also hugely damaging for a country's economic well-being. Funds that were intended for economic development, infrastructure, or any manner of public spending are diverted into the pockets of increasingly wealthy and powerful individuals. The UN estimates that corruption cheats the continent out of about $50 billion every year. Corruption occurs in every country in the world, but in Africa it is known to be particularly widespread. That's why the African Union named 2018 the year for "Winning the Fight Against Corruption."

On the other hand, some people have suggested that a number of checks and balances have been incorporated into the tribal systems, and that these can ensure a fairer distribution of wealth and power across a country. Nigeria, for example, as we've seen, has sharply delineated ethnic and religious divides. Many regions are overwhelmingly dominated by one group or another, and while the south of the country is predominantly Christian, the north is mostly Muslim. The south enjoys higher literacy rates, better health, and more money. The country's political map runs along similar lines. The result is an unwritten rule to even out any discrimination or imbalance of power across the country as a whole: the presidency (which controls most of the budget) will alternate between a Christian and a Muslim. This is an example at the highest level, but many parliaments and governments make decisions taking into account the effect they will have on the country's various tribes, with the aim of avoiding unrest and dissatisfaction. If the political parties representing tribes A, B, and C do not bear in mind the views of tribe D, they can expect trouble from that part of the country. This is similar to the workings of any other political system, but in Africa it is more tribally/ethnically based than most.

Some countries have had more success than others in limiting
the political effects of these ethnic and tribal divisions. Kwame
Nkrumah of Ghana, for example, outlawed parties based on tribal
affinity, and in Ivory Coast Félix Houphouët-Boigny, president
from 1960 to 1993, shared out power to a degree that kept a lid
on regional tensions. Botswana has been relatively stable, partially
because it is one of the few African states with a high degree of
homogeneity, plus a democratic system and a functioning economy. Tanzania is another exception, despite having more than a
hundred tribes. Its first president, Julius Nyerere, insisted that
to forge a national identity the sole national language would be
Swahili. Already widely used in the country, it became the glue
that held together a nation. But even Tanzania is showing slight
fractures: Islamists in Zanzibar are now calling for a referendum
to end the union of Tanganyika and Zanzibar that created Tanzania in 1964.

How much might tribalism affect the development of any
country in which it has a strong hold? It is probably impossible to
gauge accurately because we don't have an example of a tribe-free
country to use in comparison. Nevertheless, it is safe to say that
the need to constantly balance the competing claims of overlap-
ping groups is a distraction from the development of the state as
a single entity. When conflicts descend into violence, they can
certainly destabilize an entire country, disrupt its economy, force
millions from their homes, and cause millions of casualties. They
can be incredibly costly, both to the country as a whole and to
individual citizens, and they play a part in the terrible cycles of
poverty and inequality that occur across the continent.

Africa is the poorest continent in the world. Globalization has
lifted hundreds of millions of people out of poverty, but the gap
between the rich and the not rich has widened. The division is

particularly stark in Africa, where seven of the ten most unequal countries are to be found. Across the continent are modern cities, rapidly filling with skyscrapers, multinational companies, and a growing middle class. But in all these burgeoning urban centers, alongside the wealthy live the incredibly poor, who might be scraping by on less than $2 a day. A World Bank study in 2016 found that the percentage of Africans living in poverty had declined from 56 percent in 1990 to 43 percent in 2012, but the number of people living in those conditions had actually increased from 280 million to 330 million due to the growth in population.

Zimbabwe is among the poorer countries in Africa, and large numbers of the population are intent on finding a better life elsewhere, especially in its two much wealthier neighbors—Botswana and South Africa—to the south. However, richer countries don't necessarily want a huge influx of poor migrants, many of whom struggle to cross the borders. Botswana has a three-hundred-mile-long electric fence along its border with Zimbabwe. It says this is to stop the spread of foot-and-mouth disease in cattle, but unless Zimbabwean cows can do the high jump, it's difficult to see why the fence needs to be so high. Zimbabwe, and its impoverished population, is also fenced off from South Africa. As one of the richest countries in southern Africa, South Africa is a magnet for migrants—which is partly why it also has a fence along its border with Mozambique.

Despite these barriers, many people do cross over into South Africa, and high levels of immigration have caused tensions just as they have elsewhere in the world. In 2017 Nigeria's leadership appealed to the South African government to intervene to stop what it called "xenophobic attacks" during a spate of anti-immigrant violence, following comments reportedly made by the Zulu king, Goodwill Zwelithini kaBhekuzulu, that foreigners should "pack their bags" and go. He said he was misquoted, but the damage was done, and many of those rioting were heard chanting

"The king has spoken." The community of Zimbabweans, 3 million strong, was among the main targets, but around eight hundred thousand Nigerians are also in South Africa, and during the trouble no foreigner was safe if found by the mob. Nigerian homes and individuals were attacked, some Nigerian-owned small businesses were looted and burned, several people died, and hundreds of people were forced from their homes and fled to camps set up by the government. The trouble also led to anti–South African demonstrations in Nigeria in which South African businesses were attacked amid calls for South Africans to "go home."

Here we see a scenario familiar in countries across the world: fear and anger directed at immigrants, who are not only accused of taking local jobs but also of creating higher levels of crime by selling drugs, forming gangs, and so on. Crime isn't necessarily linked to immigration, but it is linked to poverty, and both are widespread across Africa. Statistics show that Africa is second only to the Americas in crime rates, especially murder. A UN report on global crime rates showed that of 437,000 murders in 2012, 36 percent were in the Americas and 31 percent in Africa. By comparison, just 5 percent of murders were committed in Europe. The same report suggested that in some parts of Africa the murder rate was increasing.

Poverty appears to be both a cause of crime and a consequence of it, and poor people are caught in this cycle. Most of those living desperate lives in shantytowns do not turn to crime despite lacking access to what better-off people would regard as the basics of a comfortable life. Nevertheless, they suffer the consequences of crime—theft, violence, weapons, gangs, drug selling, overstretched law enforcement, exploitation—all of which loop back into insecurity and underdevelopment and thus help sustain the poverty into which they were born.

While the poor are trapped in this cycle, the rich are getting richer and using their wealth to save themselves from experiencing the hardships of day-to-day poverty by retreating behind walls of their own: the gated community, a clear sign of the economic divisions and the vast inequality that can be found across Africa. Here are many attractions, as one advertisement makes clear: "Uncomplicate your life! Escape to Lusaka's newest suburb. An exclusive and secure residential estate . . . MukaMunya is protected by an alarmed electric fence, a gated entrance and a 24-hour security system allowing entry by invitation only. . . . The main road is tarred too, making that dream of driving a low-slung executive car an option. Enjoy a host of facilities. . . . The park club house offers two tennis courts, a squash court, a 25-metre swimming pool and a fully stocked bar. In close proximity to one of Lusaka's finest schools, the 'equestrian belt' and an easy drive into town." The walls of a gated community promise luxury, safety, and exclusivity. If your name's not on the list, you can't come in, and to get on the list you have to pay. A lot. *MukaMunya* means "my place" in Soli, one of the Bantu languages of Zambia, but most of the local population can but dream of having a home there.

Fortified communities are not exactly new. From early agricultural times, on through the Roman period and the Middle Ages, walls around collections of dwellings were a normal way of living. Only in relatively recent times—with the rise of the nation-state and internal security, including police forces—did cities allow walls to be taken down or begin to expand outside them. Now the walls have started to go back up. But whereas in the past the whole community could retreat behind its walls for protection, now only a minority live behind walls permanently.

The trend for living in gated communities started to reemerge during the twentieth century and has been gathering pace ever since. Now such communities are being built across the length and breadth of Africa, with Zambia, South Africa, Kenya, and Nigeria leading the way. South Africa pioneered the African gated trend. According to the *Economist*, as early as 2004 Johannesburg alone had three hundred enclosed neighborhoods and twenty security estates, while in 2015 Graça Machel, widow of Nelson Mandela, inaugurated the "parkland residence" Steyn City—a development four times the size of Monaco—which includes South Africa's most expensive house.

This is not limited to Africa. In the USA, for example, the use of "fortified towns" seems to have begun in California in the 1930s with gated enclaves such as the Rolling Hills estate. Some scholars identify an acceleration in the building of gated communities in the 1980s and suggest that as governments cut back on welfare and spent less on communal areas the people who could afford to do so withdrew from the public space. One study in 1997 estimated that by then the USA had twenty thousand gated communities housing 3 million residents.

Similar patterns are clear in Latin America, which has also seen a dramatic rise in "fortress communities" this century. In Lima, Peru, what has become known as the Wall of Shame separates one of the wealthiest neighborhoods of the city from one of the poorest. Some gated communities have grown to be almost cities within cities—Alphaville in São Paulo, Brazil, for instance, houses more than thirty thousand—completely changing the way the urban centers operate and are organized. The Chinese are building developments far exceeding the scope of Alphaville.

This modern way of living is not only for the very rich either. The rapid growth of the middle class in many African countries has led to the development of gated developments marketed at those who cannot afford the luxury of a top-end detached house, but who can pay for a flat in a large compound of modern high-rise buildings. Take Nigeria, for example: in its former capital, Lagos, which has a population of 21 million, you can find some of the world's poorest people, living in the slums in floating shanty-towns on the city's lagoons, or crammed onto the islands around the mainland, close to multimillion-dollar mansions. In the new upmarket developments it is not unusual to see a two-bedroom apartment on the market for more than $1 million. You certainly wouldn't get any change from a million if you bought in one of the developing new "cities" such as Eko Atlantic, which is built on just under four square miles of land reclaimed from the bottom of the Atlantic Ocean adjacent to Lagos. The city is ringed with such developments. They are a testament to the burgeoning middle and upper middle class of this oil-rich country of 186 million people, and how wealth distribution is changing in its urban areas.

The boom in such properties is partly a response to high crime rates, as we've seen. However, ironically, a 2014 study published in the *Journal of Housing and the Built Environment* suggested that moving to a house inside the "fortress" might actually increase your chances of a break-in. Anyone well-off enough to live in a gated community is assumed by burglars to have something worth stealing.

The 2014 study did acknowledge that the compounds offer levels of protection higher in general than those outside them, but said that they leave public spaces deserted and at higher risk of crime. Gated communities threaten to weaken social cohesion wherever they are built. The wealthy have always lived in certain parts of cities, but have shared social spaces, be they town squares, markets, parks, or entertainment areas that are open to everyone. The new model of urban and suburban living is designed to be exclusionary: you can only get to the town square if you can get through the security surrounding the town. This lack of interaction may shrink the sense of civic engagement, encourage groupthink among those on the inside, and lead to a psychological division, with poorer people left feeling like outsiders, as though they've been walled off. Increased wealth without bringing a relative degree of prosperity to all reinforces division.

Gated areas have consequences for the entire community and have further effects on attitudes to both local and national governments. If significant numbers of people live in communities in which they pay private companies to provide the infrastructure, such as water pipes and roads, and to protect them with private police and fire agencies, while dealing only with private health care, then the role of local and national government diminishes. And if a government's remit is only to administer smaller sectors of society, then the cohesion of the nation-state is also weakened. It would be hard in this scenario for a politician to come up with the slogan Britain's David Cameron used in 2016 in relation to financial hardships—"We're all in it together."

Or, to put it in the language of the United Nations in its UN-Habitat report: "Impacts of gating are seen in the real and potential spatial and social fragmentation of cities, leading to the diminished use and availability of public space and increased socioeconomic polarization. In this context, gating has been characterized as having counterintuitive impacts, even increasing crime and the fear of crime as the middle classes abandon public streets to the vulnerable poor, to street children and families, and to the offenders who prey on them." However, some studies suggest that within the compounds gating has helped encourage a sense of social cohesion and community neighborhood that transcends tribe and ethnicity. This is where the tribal concept based on ethnicity breaks down.

In a 2015 study on gated communities in Ghana, when residents were asked why they had chosen to live in the developments, the top response was "quality homes," with "safety and security" second and "class of residents" third. A "sense of community" was sixth, and a hint of the impact of gated communities on culture came in eighth: "a buffer from extended family system." Although this reason came eighth, it was a fascinating insight into how this modern reinterpretation of a walled city will slowly contribute to the weakening of the close extended family ties found throughout the continent.

In places where welfare provided by the state is weak, and where employment is often temporary and informal, one or two relatively high-earning family members will normally use their income to help support dozens of extended-family members. Giving a family member a job is not considered nepotism but a family responsibility. This has long been the case in Africa, so putting a physical barrier between members of the extended family will have a negative effect as most of the properties built are for the nuclear, not the larger, family. The developments are a different world, and not just in the physical sense. For those on the inside, the new, much looser "tribe" is the social class of your immediate neighbors.

The new tribes living behind the walls identify with each other because they have things worth stealing, not because their mothers and fathers originally came from a certain region or spoke a particular language. They have similar lifestyles, often similar interests, which are similarly protected. When you have enough money, you can pay others to protect you; when you don't, you band together, and so behind the walls the sense of "we" or "us" is diluted, sometimes to as little as "I."

Ethnic identity still predominates in most African countries. While the nation-state borders are real—they exist within a legal framework and are sometimes marked by some sort of physical barrier—they do not always exist in the minds of people living within and around them. Like the Sahrawi, whose traditional territory has been split by the Moroccan Wall, many still feel the pull of their ancestral lands.

The postcolonial consensus by African leaders not to change the borders was based on a fear that to do so would invite never-ending conflict, and in the hope that they could build genuine nation-states and thus reduce ethnic divisions. It has been incredibly difficult, not least because in Africa the nations still frequently cross nation-state borders, whereas in, for example, Western Europe, clear geographical or linguistic lines more often mark where one nation-state ends and another begins.

We are now well into the twenty-first century, and Africa stands at a point that, with hindsight, was always coming: it needs to balance the rediscovery of its precolonial senses of nationhood with the realities of the current functioning nation-states. That's a fine line, fraught with danger, but to ignore or deny the divisions that occur across the length and breadth of this vast space will not make them go away.

Once there was the "scramble for Africa"; now there is a race to bring about a degree of prosperity so that people may be persuaded to live peacefully together while simultaneously working on solutions where they wish to live apart.

CHAPTER 7

Europe

Today, no walls can separate humanitarian or human rights crises in one part of the world from national security crises in another. What begins with the failure to uphold the dignity of one life all too often ends with a calamity for entire nations.

—Kofi Annan

Previous pages: People gather at the Berlin Wall as it starts to come down, November 1989.

Early one gray morning in 1979 I boarded a military train in West Germany heading through East Germany to Charlottenburg station in the West German sector of Berlin. The city was formerly the capital of a united Germany but was now locked within East Germany. By that time the wall had been up for eighteen years, and it appeared to be a permanent fixture in our lives, which would keep us apart forever. There didn't seem to be any prospect of living another way—the present was fixed in concrete, barbed wire, part of a conflict that threatened to split enough atoms to kill us all.

As a serving member of the RAF, I was armed with a military ID card and thus had no need of a passport for this journey. At the East German border we stopped at a station complete with barbed-wire fences and a watchtower. Terse, unsmiling Soviet border guards entered the train and checked our documents while the East German Transport Police, known as TraPos, used sniffer dogs to inspect the underside of the carriages. The capitalist locomotive and crew were replaced by good Communist versions, and after about two hours we chugged our way into the military corridor linking West Germany to West Berlin.

The carriage doors had been locked with chains from the outside, and the windows were sealed as we entered a shabby, drab, half-lit world in which reality seemed to be a permanent gray. We were forbidden to stand up when the train stopped at stations or to speak to any East German or Soviet officials or civilians. The length of the 145-mile corridor was enclosed by

high wire fences interspersed with watchtowers complete with
floodlights and guards with submachine guns. Behind the fences
were cleared "killing zones," allowing a clear line of fire in case
anyone was brave—or foolish—enough to try to cross the border.
After a clanking, stop-start, four-hour journey, we rolled into
Berlin and toward the symbol of the greatest ideological divide
of the twentieth century. This was a city wall like no other—built
not to repel invaders, but to keep people in.

These days most Europeans take the idea of freedom of movement for granted. But it was not so long ago that travel across the
Continent was severely restricted. During the Cold War, to cross
borders in Western Europe you had to have a passport, but it was
routine. Crossing the Iron Curtain into Eastern Europe required
a passport, paperwork, and security checks and was done in the
knowledge that your every movement would be monitored. The
Iron Curtain and the Berlin Wall were the stark physical reminders
that a continent with a shared history, interlinked cultures, and
ancient trading routes had been completely riven by ideology
and Great Power politics.

In the aftermath of World War II, as the Communist and
capitalist victors sized each other up across this new divide, the
Soviet economic system quickly started to fail its citizens. Just
by looking out a window or crossing a street, ordinary people
in the East could see the spectacularly successful rebuilding of
West Germany. West German TV reached most of East Germany, beaming images of a burgeoning consumer society into
ordinary people's homes. The East Germans even used to joke
that the most easterly regions, out of range of the West German
transmitters, were the "Valleys of the Clueless." Every day that
people were able to witness the progress was a blow to the idea
that the Soviet system was superior. The ruling Socialist Unity
Party of Germany had boasted in 1958 that its principal task was
to overtake West Germany in the consumption of consumer goods

within two years. This didn't happen, but the Soviet Union did take the lead in the space race; a popular East German parody of a Communist slogan of the time went *"Ohne Butter, ohne Sahne, auf dem Mond die rote Fahne"* (There's no butter, there's no cream, but on the moon the red flag flutters).

Before the wall went up, so many East Berliners had opted to migrate to the Western sectors, either to work or live permanently, that the East German economy was in dire straits. About 2 million had voted with their feet in the previous decade, and the flow was increasing. Between January 1960 and the end of July 1961 another 330,000 people moved West. East Germany was losing its workforce and its credibility.

In the middle of the night of August 13, 1961, with Moscow's approval, the East German army began to wall off half of one of the world's great capital cities. The authorities on one side called it the Antifaschistischer Schutzwall (antifascist protection bulwark); those on the other called it "the wall of shame." For the first few years it consisted of occasional stretches of wall, but mostly of blocked-off streets, walled-up windows, and stretches of barbed wire. But within a decade a concrete wall was reinforced by watchtowers, bunkers, electric fences, dogs, automatic shooting ranges, and hundreds of armed guards.

On the eastern side people were forbidden to approach it, but in the West you could walk up streets that ended where the wall was built and touch the illogical madness of the division of the German and European peoples. On this side, the black humor of the Cold War years could be spray-painted on the wall. I remember two examples of the graffiti, both in English: JUMP OVER THE WALL AND JOIN THE PARTY and WARNING! EAST GERMAN HIGH JUMP TRAINING AREA. No one could jump the wall, but tens of thousands tried other ways of crossing from East to West, and at least 140 people were killed in the attempt, although some researchers put the total much higher. Tunnels seemed the most obvious escape route, but other memorable and successful efforts were made.

Just four months after the wall went up, twenty-eight-year-old train driver Harry Deterling pointed the passenger train he was driving at the wall, opened the throttle, and smashed through the fortifications. By no coincidence six members of his family were among the passengers. Two years later Horst Klein, an acrobat, noticed that a disused steel cable stretched over the border. Sixty feet above the guards patrolling below, he inched, hand over hand, to West Berlin. Perhaps the most audacious and brilliant escape came in 1979. Hans Strelczyk and Gunter Wetzel used their mechanical knowledge to build a rudimentary hot-air balloon using propane cylinders. Their wives fashioned the balloon bag from canvas and bedsheets. Gathering their four children (and having tested the wind direction), they floated up to eight thousand feet and several miles westward to freedom.

Nevertheless, the wall, judged by its raison d'être, can be called a success. It is estimated that only around five thousand got across it; the mass exodus had been halted. The East German economy began to stabilize after its workforce was imprisoned, and by the mid-1960s the state had control over its trade and currency and was capable of functioning, along with the rest of the Russian empire's vassal states.

However, the East Germans had not been given a choice, and most of them knew it. They were trapped behind a wall that both physically and mentally imprisoned several generations. Shortly after it went up, psychologists and psychiatrists began to use the term *wall disease* (*Mauerkrankheit*). The barrier, it was theorized, created a syndrome in which some people considered themselves locked up, which led to psychological and behavioral disorders such as schizophrenia, alcoholism, depression, and even suicide. The Swiss psychoanalyst Carl Jung took a wider view, arguing that the Iron Curtain meant Europe in general was "dissociated like a neurotic."

Some degree of mental illness would have been present anyway, but it's also difficult to believe that the wall had no hand in this.

Europe during the Cold War (1947–89), divided by the Iron Curtain.

For those of us in the West, the East was "over there"—behind the Iron Curtain. Several generations of thinkers and intellectuals were convinced that the East German system was superior to that of the West in both economic and moral terms. When the blindingly obvious became apparent to them in 1989, it was, and remains, difficult for some to admit that a lifetime of belief was based on the rubble of a giant prison system. As for the rest of us, we didn't go "inter-railing" on our summer holidays to visit Budapest, Dresden, and Warsaw, nor were there weekend visits to Prague or Tallinn. Most of us were in our thirties before we ever met anyone from "over there" because it was difficult to get there—and nigh on impossible for them to get "here." Many people behind the Iron Curtain needed a permit to travel from one city to another within their own country, never mind cross an international border to the West. For twenty-eight years it was just the way it was. And then, suddenly, it wasn't.

In 1985 Mikhail Gorbachev had become general secretary of the Communist Party of the Soviet Union. Slowly he began loosening the chains around people's lives. The word *perestroika* began to be used, meaning "restructuring," but also signifying "listening." Within this came the idea of *glasnost*, or "openness." In a thousand small ways society and politics opened up and people listened to one another. By late spring 1989 the idea had spread so far that Hungary, behind the Iron Curtain, had begun to dismantle part of its border fence with Austria. That summer thousands of East Germans decided to take their summer holidays in Hungary.

By August hundreds of East German families were camped outside the West German consulate in Budapest, and hundreds more had taken refuge on the grounds of Holy Family Church, all under the watchful eye of officers from East German state security—the Stasi. A rumor went around about a "Pan-European Picnic" to be held at the Austrian border, and people were suddenly on the move. By late afternoon on August 19 several hundred had gathered by a wooden gate; dozens moved toward it, then hundreds ran through the gap, some crying with joy, some laughing, and some simply continuing to run, unable to believe they were really across the border. Three weeks later Hungary fully opened the border crossings, and sixty thousand people flooded out. The German chancellor, Helmut Kohl, said later, "It was in Hungary that the first stone was removed from the Berlin Wall."

In the autumn, mass antigovernment demonstrations took place in East Germany. In October, the country's much-loathed leader,

Erich Honecker, resigned and was replaced by the marginally less loathed Egon Krenz. Without guidance from its Russian masters, the politburo was making policy on the hoof. It decided to allow East Berliners to apply for travel visas to visit West Germany. This process could have been managed, and the Communist authorities might have been able to buy time and engineer ways of staying in control, but one of those small details that can change history got in the way. The man tasked with announcing the visa decision on November 9 was the minister of propaganda, Günter Schabowski. He had just returned from holiday, had not attended the meeting at which the policy was decided, and had no idea of any of the details of the process, which included briefings for border guard commanders the following day so they could follow orders. When he was asked, "When do the new regulations begin?," he hesitated, then replied, "As far as I know, immediately, right now." Thousands of East Berliners were already at the wall; within hours tens of thousands of people were gathered on both sides.

At first the East German border guards refused to allow anyone out, but then, amid the confusion, they stamped a few passports and then stood back to allow the crowds to surge through. The scenes, which a year before no one had predicted, were amazing. West and East Germans embraced one another, champagne corks popped, and the "wall peckers," ordinary East and West Berliners, climbed to the top of the wall with chisels, hammers, and axes and set to work leveling the great barrier. The word of the night was *wahnsinnig*—"mind-blowing."

It was a heady, emotional day for all Europeans. I was living in Paris at the time and about thirty-six hours later saw a battered old East Berlin Trabant car, with four young East Berliners inside, sputtering up the Champs-Élysées. With the border open, they had decided the first thing they wanted to do was see the City of Light and had driven almost nonstop to get there. All along the great avenue Parisians stopped to applaud their German neighbors and the new era.

The two Germanys united politically in 1990, after forty-five years apart. In 1989 Willy Brandt, the former chancellor of West Germany, was reported as saying, "Now what belongs together will grow together." It was assumed that he was referring to Germany, though in fact he was talking about Europe in general.

So, a united Germany? A united Europe? Up to a point. The divide that chisels and hammers could not destroy remained—"the wall in the heads." The wall hadn't just prevented people from traveling, it had created deep gulfs—economic, political, and social—that would prove harder to overcome than the physical barrier. So, after the tears of joy and the declarations of brotherhood, the hard yards of reunification began. This was not a merger of equals. In 1990 the East had a population of 16.1 million, the West 63.7 million, and the West's economy dwarfed that of the East. Armed with the mandate from unified elections, which had seen the former Communist Party in the East crushed, the capitalist, democratic Western system set about destroying the Communist machine.

All large countries have regional cultural differences, but in this large country the people had had no contact with one another and lived under different systems. For example, in the West belief in God and church attendance were declining slowly, whereas in the East it had become a relic of the past. The East Germans may have rejected Communism, but that didn't mean they were prepared for the harsher, more selfish aspects of capitalism. On the other side, West Germans may have welcomed unification, but quickly began to grumble at the financial cost of absorbing a failed economy and a population that needed to be "reeducated" in the ways of the modern world.

It all boiled down to a German version of "us and them"—*Ossis* (Easties) and *Wessis* (Westies). Opinion polls in 2004 found that one in eight East Germans hankered after the old days before the wall came down, and in 1999 many East Germans still spoke about feeling humiliated by job losses, compulsory retraining programs, and their difficulties with the new system and consumer culture. Even in 2015, a study by the Berlin Institute for Population and Development concluded that at least half of all Germans still felt the difference in both economic and cultural terms. The eastern areas are often still referred to as "the new federal states," which is a reminder that, to some people, the East was joining the West, as opposed to the two joining equally.

Despite investment of more than $2 trillion, the eastern regions remain poorer than the West, and in late 2017 unemployment there was 12 percent, double that of the West. This is not a story of failure: the East has become considerably richer and more efficient than it was—Dresden, Leipzig, and other cities are thriving, living standards have risen. But more than a quarter of a century after unification, the divisions remain. Out of Germany's twenty most prosperous cities, Jena is the only one in the East that makes the list. This is not only because wages are lower there; it is also because, due to the Communist system, property ownership was low. At unification, any savings people had were converted at the rate of two East marks to one West mark.

In 2010, sociologists at Bielefeld University found that although those from the East composed about 20 percent of the population, less than 5 percent of people the researchers defined as the "elite" in politics, business, and the media were from the East, even though education levels are higher there, especially in math and science—thanks in part to the high level of investment in schools since reunification. That education gap has itself meant that the brightest from the eastern region head west to take the best-paying jobs. With females achieving higher educational standards than males, the ratio of young women to men has fallen in the East, with a concurrent drop in the birth rate there. Long-term relationships and marriage between people from the East and West were once unusual, but have now begun to appear. Nevertheless, the majority of these comprise men from the West and women from the East; that they are still far from the norm is shown by the nickname for an *Ossi/Wessi* couple—*Wossis*. All this has contributed to a shrinking population in eastern Germany, although the rate has slowed. Some reports suggest the decline may even have stopped, partly thanks to the success of cities such as Dresden and Leipzig ("Germany's coolest city"), although this has come at the expense of an exodus of young people from rural areas.

Regional differences in culture, in both food and consumer goods, have played a role in the German postunification identity. Twenty-five years ago the East Germans flooded into shops that sold Levi's jeans, video recorders, and quality chocolate. But the consumption of the "new" products again underlined the dominance of the western side of the new joint relationship. Few East German products made it into the supermarkets in the West, and the puttering, spluttering "Trabbie" became the subject of Pan-European humor. The Trabant jokes have gone (as have many of the factories producing the old eastern goods), and the cultural and regional differences become less political as the years pass, but even in 2010 national headlines were made when Chancellor Merkel, an *Ossi*, was asked about her favorite food and chose an East German meat-and-pickle soup of Russian origin known as *solyanka*. Over time local foods such as solyanka and the Spreewald cucumber will simply be an element of regional culinary identity, with no political tang. There is no going back as *Ostalgie* (a mix of "nostalgia" and "east") fades.

The divides in modern Germany are nowhere near as stark as they were during the Cold War, and some are due to factors that predate the Communist/capitalist split. However, the outlines of the Berlin Wall and the Iron Curtain can still be seen—and can still be felt. You can see physical remnants along Bernauer Strasse, at the Niederkirchnerstrasse, by the Bundestag (the federal parliament), and at the Wall Museum at what was Checkpoint Charlie. At flea markets you can even buy a bit of concrete "chiseled out of the wall on that famous night in 1989," although the chances of its being genuine are slim given that the volume sold would have made the wall one of the biggest structures ever erected. Either way, you can take home a little gray symbol of history, of human suffering, of the ultimate political division of the twentieth century that split Europe in a way that seems unimaginable to many people nowadays.

After the wall came down, things moved fast in Europe. When the East Europeans came in from the cold and the Germans reunited, the political consensus was that the future belonged to a unified, borderless Europe, with a single currency in which the nation-state would fade away. This EU federation would interact with other major blocs in a globalized world dominated by huge trading pacts. People, goods, services, and money would all move freely between the member states.

The EU's founding fathers helped rebuild a shattered and divided Europe after World War II, based on restoring the nation-states to prosperity within a shared trading area; hence it was originally called the European Economic Community. Their descendants took the view that the European states could be built into one unified nation tied together by ideology. This noble aspiration is rooted in the desire to end two thousand years of European tribes warring against one another. In the 1990s Yugoslavia discovered too late that it had failed to extinguish the flames of Balkan nationalism under the blanket of Slavic socialism and watched as the entire house burned down. Those seeking a European superstate saw Yugoslavia as evidence of precisely why the EU project had to succeed. However, a variety of small details and a few large-scale, high-impact factors have exposed problems in the system.

When the community of nation-states began to morph into a union of member states in the 1980s, more and more powers were transferred to Brussels in a dilution of sovereignty that not everyone supported. Over the years countries have called for more independence and the ability to make decisions in the best interests of their own populations on budgets, laws, trading regulations, and so on. They don't want to be dictated to by a centralized power in Brussels. Following EU directives has led to serious economic issues in some countries. The Single European Act of 1986 established a single market, and a single currency, the euro, was created in 1999. However, no single fiscal or financial policy was concurrent, nor did the euro system have the flexibility to absorb regional financial shocks. When times were good, people were less inclined to question the wisdom of creating this interdependent system. Now, however, the euro sometimes struggles to hold its own in the world markets and can fluctuate alarmingly; and there have been financial winners and losers. Greece, for example, suffers horrendous levels of youth unemployment, partially due to economic policies forced upon it by Berlin and Brussels.

The EU has also faced the challenge of uniting East and West Europe, after expanding in 2004 to allow in several of the eastern states. Freedom of movement is one of the ideals of the EU, giving Europeans the right to live, work, and travel throughout the member countries. It was intended both to enable growth across Europe and to encourage integration among the European populations. Many have embraced the ideal, traveling around the Continent in a way that wouldn't have been possible just a few decades ago, especially to places previously hidden behind the Iron Curtain. This has helped reduce that sense of "the other" that was pervasive during the Cold War. But, just as Germany has experienced a lasting impact from the Berlin Wall, many differences remain between the West and the East. States such as Hungary, Poland, and Bulgaria had been subjected to the same travel restrictions and economic lapses as East Germany, and their economies were then severely disrupted by the collapse of the Soviet Union. Progress has been made, but many of the EU's poorest countries area those that used to be in the Eastern Bloc.

The expansion of the European Union since it was originally formed.

When the eastern states were incorporated into the EU, GDP per capita in countries such as the UK and France was almost six times higher than in Poland. Despite this, many in the political class in West European countries severely underestimated how many people would move westward to find work and were unprepared when several million did just that. Migrant workers are required and often do jobs some of the indigenous populations reject. However, the hard logic of economics does not always persuade French, Dutch, or British plumbers, builders, or taxi drivers of the benefits to their country of migrant labor when they find themselves in competition with new arrivals for jobs, housing, and health care. When so many economic migrants began to travel from poor European countries to rich ones, people started to grumble at the influx of East European migrant workers and question the benefits of free movement. This was felt most strongly in Britain with the rise of the UK Independence Party (UKIP) and ultimately contributed to the Brexit vote.

Adding to this growing discontent was the financial crash of 2008 and subsequent government cuts in social spending and investment across the EU. While the banks were crumbling, the taxpayers in each nation-state were left to clean up the mess. With unemployment rising and migration increasing across a border-free region, the weaknesses of the system started to show. True believers will endorse the European project come what may, ardent nationalists will always fight against it, but agnostics will only support it if it works for them—and large parts of the European electorate started to feel that it was no longer delivering. Without economic prosperity to bind them together, and with waning support for a failing system, rising levels of nationalism could no longer be suppressed or ignored.

The EU has never succeeded in replacing the nation-state in the hearts of most Europeans. It could be argued that its founders moved too fast, and too arrogantly, in believing that the creation of Europe would result in a population whose identification was European first, nation-state second. In 1861, one of the pioneers of Italian unification, Massimo d'Azeglio, said, "We have made Italy; now we must make Italians." Even that has proved a challenge and is still ongoing; this was the case even where the regions had a shared religion, history, and, to an extent, geography. To create the EU and the eurozone and then set about making Europeans is an infinitely more difficult project in which the very different interests, needs, and priorities of Finland and Hungary have to mesh with those of Greece and Portugal. The limited success in doing so is visible in the growing instability in the union. The Scandinavians have met to discuss the possibility of a Nordic Union should the EU collapse. The Visegrád Group (Slovakia/ Czech Republic/Poland/Hungary) increasingly presents a united front to Brussels. The push of "One Europe" is challenged by Brexit, by separatist movements in Scotland, Belgium, Italy, and Spain, and by the growth of Euroskeptic parties in almost every country. Late 2017 brought this into sharp focus with the crisis in Catalonia, underlining the tensions that exist when several nations are within a state.

Many academics like to argue that nationalism is a "false construct" because it is based on "imagined communities," but there is nothing false about people's feelings concerning their national identity, and "imagined" does not mean nonexistent. The Palestinians, for example, through language, religion, and culture, have developed a strong sense of identity and thus believe that they are a nation and deserving of a state. Few academics challenge this narrative, yet intellectually they continue to argue that nationalism is outdated, even primitive. The latter claim may be true, but to ignore the reality of nationalism, which is found the world over, is folly. Some academics, intellectuals, and sections of the media, business, and political class see themselves as liberated from nationalism. In 2016 the European Commission president, Jean-Claude Juncker, described national borders as "the worst invention ever." He may have a point, but stating it so baldly is hardly likely to win over nationalists to his idea of a European superstate.

The new elite, of which Mr. Juncker is a prime example, doesn't seem to understand nationalism and are too quick to dismiss it.

As the late historian Tony Judt wrote in 1996, while reluctantly arguing that an ever-closer bonding of the Europeans was impossible, "We should recognize the reality of nations and states, and note the risk that, when neglected, they become an electoral resource of virulent nationalists."

That is what has happened. As nations have experienced rapid change due to migration, attitudes toward immigrants have hardened and support for virulent nationalist parties has grown. A majority of people in most West European countries still have a favorable view of newcomers, but most opinion polls taken since 2004 track declining support. That trend has only intensified with the sudden influx of non-European refugees and migrants across both East and West Europe, fueled by the turmoil in the Middle East and beyond. The pressure of this latest challenge, given that the EU was already struggling to unify its members, who were still reeling from the effects of the financial crisis, has exacerbated cracks that have started to appear in the EU edifice from the Baltic to the Mediterranean and is threatening the system.

The migrant crisis built up steadily from 2011, hitting a peak in 2015. With serious conflicts and civil wars across the Middle East and Africa, millions have been killed and displaced, and millions more have fled the violence, looking for a new life in the West. At first most European leaders were welcoming, but as more and more refugees kept coming, it became clear that the EU was unprepared to handle such numbers—over a million in 2015 alone—and that a growing number of people were becoming increasingly unwilling to do so. As attitudes began to change, certain borders within the EU started to tighten again as many countries sought to regain control over the number of immigrants crossing their boundaries.

Unconnected to the migrant crisis, a resurgent Russia has also played its part in the rise of the "barrier continent." Following Russia's annexation of Crimea, Ukraine began building defensive

fortifications along its eastern border. In 2015 Estonia and Latvia
started building fences on their frontiers with Russia, and in 2017
Lithuania, which had already reintroduced conscription in alarm at
Russian actions, followed their example. However, the migration
crisis, along with the Ukrainian/Russian conflict, is a major reason
why Europe now has about the same length of physical barriers
along national borders as it had during the Cold War. The situation began along the borders of the EU itself. A few places were
already fenced and walled, for example, Spain's Moroccan enclaves
of Melilla and Ceuta. In the former, as with many barriers, the
twenty-foot-high double fence has proved porous. In early 2018
at least two hundred African migrants stormed over the fence,
some so desperate that they attacked police officers trying to stop
them. Most were caught later and taken to a migrant detention
center, but thousands have made it to Spain via this route in the
past few years. One of the first new walls to go up in 2011 was a
razor-wire fence along the Greek border with Turkey to prevent
migrants and refugees from the wider Middle East and Africa
from getting in. In 2015 Bulgaria followed suit.

However, the border barriers at these entry points haven't
stopped new waves of migrants from arriving and finding a way in.
Migration paths tend to change—many people choose to make the
dangerous sea crossing from Turkey to Greece, for example—and
although a 2016 deal between the EU and Turkey saw the latter
agree to take back large numbers of these migrants, many still
find their way into the EU. In response, a number of controls
and barriers have started appearing along borders between EU
countries as well.

Hungary was one of the first; twenty-six years after the Cold
War barriers came down, new ones started to go up. It began to
build a fence, first along its border with Serbia, then the one with
Croatia, ending up with over three hundred miles of razor-wire
fencing to keep people out. During the summer of 2015, many

thousands of immigrants were crossing into Hungary every day; now that number has been reduced to virtually none. The Hungarian government has been one of the most outspoken against immigration and EU plans for resettling people. Prime Minister Viktor Orbán announced a referendum in 2016 on whether Hungarians wanted the EU to be able to dictate immigrant quotas. A vast majority voted in line with the government, although voter turnout was low. Nevertheless, a majority of the population do seem to sympathize with this viewpoint: according to a survey by the Pew Research Center, 76 percent of Hungarians think that refugees will increase terrorist incidents, and 82 percent see them as a burden on the country, taking jobs and social benefits. The Hungarian government continues to push its agenda, playing on people's fear of foreign threats and focusing on the dangers from immigration of terrorism and the spread of Islam, and tightening its immigration policies even further. Although Hungary has been widely criticized for its attitudes and policies toward migrants, sanctions have not been imposed by the EU, and the prime minister's popularity in Hungary has not been dented. Mr. Orbán won the 2018 general election with another comfortable majority.

Several other nations have followed Hungary's example and taken similar measures, and a number of "temporary" border controls have arisen, including within the "border-free" Schengen Area. Slovenia erected a fence along its border with Croatia; Macedonia along its Greek border; Austria along its busiest border crossings with Slovenia and Italy; and plans are in place to construct a wall in Calais to prevent migrants from crossing the English Channel. To the north, Norway has built a fence along its border with Russia, and Sweden began to restrict the flow of migrants entering the city of Malmö across the Øresund Bridge linking it with Denmark. Alongside the walls and fences, other countries started to tighten their borders with further measures. These are mostly designed to restrict the movement of

non-European migrants and refugees who have entered the EU
through less secure borders—and the wave of terror attacks in
recent years has helped make the idea of checks more acceptable
to many people. However, the existence of these barriers still has
an impact and threatens one of the basic ideals behind the EU.

The barriers also have a serious effect on countries where
immigrants are now stuck—especially in places where they continue to arrive. Greece, for example, has tens of thousands now
stranded on its island centers with nowhere to go, straining its
resources. With the migrant crisis affecting some countries more
than others, and with some refusing to share the burden, relations
between the EU states are further strained.

Nevertheless, huge numbers of Europeans do have a positive
view of immigration and are happy to welcome newcomers to
their countries. Many feel the West has a moral obligation to help
those fleeing violence and persecution, while others support the
argument, put forward by many politicians, economists, and business leaders, that European countries need immigrants. Due to
aging populations and low birth rates, some countries—Germany,
for example, where the median age is 46.8—face a population
decline and so need immigrants to ensure a healthy economy in
the future. But although governments repeatedly try to explain
this, people tend to base their feelings on the current situation,
not on some vague problem in the future, and the number who
support immigration is shrinking. Hence opinion polls such as
those of 2014 from the Pew Research Center finding that 86 percent of Greeks and 80 percent of Italians wanted fewer immigrants
allowed into their countries. The poll was taken as the migrant
crisis was growing, but more than a year before it reached the
peaks of 2015. As for wanting more migrants? Only 1 percent of
Greeks and 14 percent of Germans surveyed felt that way.

Many EU leaders seem to have been unprepared for the backlash against immigration. It stems from a number of reasons, as

people started to see and feel the impact on their lives of so many newcomers. Across the Continent a clear divergence was, and is, based on education. Far more people without a college education want reduced immigration, which is likely because they are often competing with immigrants from within and without the EU for low-paying jobs. Many people in this category particularly dislike being told they are bigots for feeling unsettled at the scale and pace of the change they see around them; the equation between lack of education and bigotry is seen as doubly insulting.

An increase in the number of terrorist incidents across Europe has led people to link terrorism with high levels of immigration. People fear that terrorists are coming into the EU posing as refugees and asylum seekers and can then travel freely between European nations. Some of the assailants in the November 2015 attacks on Paris had entered through migrant channels, but most attacks have been carried out by EU citizens.

Some people also feel a threat to their public services, concerned that they can't cope with the additional burden, and this also ties in with a sense of fairness. Imagine being in the waiting room of a doctor's office in, say, Hungary or France and a significant number of the people around you were not born in that country. You may well want everyone to be treated, but you may also think that you have been paying for the health system for decades whereas the person next to you hasn't. The longer you wait for your own treatment, the more likely it is that you'll think it isn't fair. These may be base instincts, but they are predictable. The EU system is set up to make it fair as many member states pay in, and the citizens of all member states can benefit no matter which state they are in. But if the person in the waiting room isn't even from a fellow EU state, the sense of injustice is, for some, intensified.

Across the EU, leaders have been looking for ways to manage the levels of immigration and discontent within the population. In 2016, Denmark introduced a bill under which asylum seekers arriving in the country with cash and jewelry could keep only ten thousand kroners' worth (about $1,600); anything above this had to be contributed toward the cost of "basic maintenance, health care and accommodation." Sentimental items such as wedding rings were exempt after comparisons were made to the treatment of Jews by Nazi Germany. Some German states and the Swiss had already, quietly, introduced similar measures, although the practice is less widespread: the Swiss, for example, only recorded 112 cases where assets were taken, out of 45,000 refugees who arrived in 2015.

In Denmark, this measure, and others in the same bill, were undoubtedly intended to assuage rising anxiety about the increasing number of refugees, the cost of taking care of them, and quite possibly to dissuade refugees from heading that way. The government had one eye on the rise in support for extreme right-wing groups. What was overlooked was that Danish law already required Danes who became unemployed and had no insurance to sell valuables up to a certain level before they could receive state support. With Denmark having welcomed twenty-one thousand asylum seekers in 2015, politicians found it increasingly difficult to sell the idea of charity to a culture steeped in the Scandinavian principle of social egalitarianism. The Danes were taking in more asylum seekers than France, despite having a population twelve times smaller—and although some critics of the new regulations were Danish, what annoyed many people was the charge that the measures were racist, and that comparisons were being made to the Nazis.

Some people also are concerned that the newcomers do not share "European values." These are difficult to define, but most people would agree that the EU countries have similar ideas about individual freedoms: gender equality, sexual equality, freedom of religion, and freedom of speech. The influx of people from cultures where these are not the norms can make people feel their own values are under threat. Across the EU nations, culture wars have broken out over the idea of multiculturalism and values. For example, should gender segregation be allowed in places of higher education? Is the full burka compatible with the French concept of *laïcité*—keeping religion out of public life? What sentences should there be for committing female genital mutilation if some citizens regard it as a cultural norm? Should free speech include allowing the propagation of beliefs such as the condemnation of certain groups of people as "the worst of creatures" as, for example, Jews and Christians are described in the Koran? Or that in religious matters a woman cannot "have authority over a man; she must be silent," as taught in the New Testament?

Europe is now home to people from all over the world. It took in hundreds of thousands of Vietnamese in the late 1970s and 1980s, large numbers of Chinese and Indians have come, and most capital cities have Latin American communities. They are all part of the mix of the new Europe to which everyone is adapting, but for many possible reasons the most difficult adjustment appears to be between non-Muslims and Muslims. One thing that seems to crop up frequently is the perception that Muslims have come in vast numbers, outnumbering local populations.

Muslims actually make up a fairly small proportion of populations across the EU. The most exhaustive study prior to the latest migrant/refugee crisis was by the Pew Research Center in 2010. It found that in the EU the largest Muslim populations are in Germany (4.8 million) and France (4.7 million). This constitutes 5.8 percent and 7.5 percent of their respective populations. The UK share was 2.9 million (4.8 percent), Sweden 430,000 (4.6 percent), and Greece 610,000 (5.3 percent). The numbers are rising—a steady 1 percent increase per decade over the last thirty years, so while 6 percent of the EU population (13 million people) were Muslim in 2010, the figure was projected to rise (prior to the mass influx of 2015) to 8 percent by 2030. But the numbers are still much lower than many people believe to be the case.

The misperception may be due to a number of reasons. For example, some representatives of Muslim communities (often self-styled) are far more vocal about religious issues than any other community and are therefore more noticeable through media coverage. However, a bigger factor is probably the highly visible concentrations of Muslims in urban centers. Approximately 20 percent of Stockholm is Muslim, 13 percent of Amsterdam, 15 percent of Brussels, and 12 percent of Cologne. Many people can easily assume from what they see around them that the rest of their country is similar. For example, a UK government report in late 2016 found that in overwhelmingly Muslim parts of northern cities such as Bradford, Muslims themselves thought the UK was well over 50 percent Muslim.

The polling from 2010 also suggests a clear divide between most of Western Europe and Southern and Eastern Europe in attitudes toward Muslims. In the south and east negative attitudes prevailed; for example 72 percent of Hungarians had an adverse view of Muslims, as did 69 percent of Italians, 66 percent of Poles, and 65 percent of Greeks. When we move north and west, clear majorities give Muslims a favorable rating. In the UK "only" 28 percent of respondents had a negative attitude; in Germany this was 29 percent.

However, in some parts of Western Europe, anti-Muslim sentiments seem to be on the rise. Public anxiety about Islam is probably highest in France. In the 2010 poll, for example, only 29 percent of people had a negative attitude toward Muslims, but hostility has since steadily increased, which may be linked both to the wave of terror attacks France has suffered and to increased migration. An Ipsos survey in *Le Monde* titled "French Fractures 2017" found that 60 percent of respondents "believe the religion of Islam is incompatible with the values of the French Republic."

On immigration, 65 percent said too many foreigners were in France. On this point a political split in attitudes was clear—95 percent of National Front voters agreed as opposed to 46 percent of socialists. A few months earlier, the then president, François Hollande, was one of that 46 percent. In a book titled *A Président Shouldn't Say That*, he is quoted as having remarked, "I think there are too many arrivals, immigrants who shouldn't be there." He also acknowledged that France has a "problem with Islam. . . . Nobody doubts that."

France certainly has a problem with integration. Whole swathes of French towns and cities are now overwhelmingly Muslim. The neighborhoods tend to be on the periphery of the urban areas and are almost always among the poorest parts of town. We have been here before. Substitute some of the words in this fascinating 1928 essay by Charles Lambert in *Foreign Affairs* magazine, and it could have been written in 2018:

> The foreigners who migrate to France tend also to congregate together, and certain of our departments have become veritable centers of *irredentism*. Several villages in the Département du Nord are peopled entirely by Poles who have brought their wives, their children, their priests and their schoolmasters along with them. Immigrants from Poland make up 20 per cent of the population of Lens, 40 per cent of the population of Courrières, 68 per cent of the population of Ostricourt. Thirty thousand Italians have settled in the south-west. The conquest of our frontier provinces by a process of infiltration is proceeding systematically. In the Riviera district nearly a third of the whole population is foreign, while the proportion reaches almost a half in Nice.

These communities ended up being assimilated, and this may happen again with the growing Muslim populations. However, there are differences—ones that apply to the European experience of the latest waves of immigration as a whole. First, if we accept that racism still exists across the Continent, then the skin color of most European Muslims may hold them back, both socially and economically. Second, unlike the Polish and Italian communities of the 1920s, some voices within the Muslim communities are telling them that they have come to an abominable place that must be resisted. These preachers of hate, often expounding an extreme religious worldview, may not represent the majority, but in communities in which faith plays a central role they have a platform and influence greater than their white extreme right-wing counterparts. Immigrant communities often have difficulty in settling in unfamiliar surroundings and gaining the acceptance of the native population, and this struggle is compounded if some of the communities' "leaders" are telling them to embrace separation.

Negative perceptions of "outsiders" have caused divisions not just between countries, but also within communities, political parties, the media, at street level, and in the courts in every EU country. Free movement was already a challenge when it merely concerned Europeans, but real discontent was limited, to an extent, to the fringes of society. The arrival of so many non-Europeans has helped ignite the simmering nationalism across the EU countries and is a major factor in the dramatic rise of the Far Right in the last few years. A decade ago the only European extreme right-wing party (other than those of their own country) that most people could name was probably the French National Front. Now several are familiar throughout Europe, among them Golden Dawn (Greece), Sweden Democrats, Party for Freedom (Netherlands), Freedom Party (Austria), and Jobbik (Hungary). Most of the ultranationalist parties are against further EU integration, but a central tenet for all of them is a fear of Islam, and this is clearly a driving force for many of their supporters. The nationalists argue that they are simply against Islamism in the form of radical political Islam, but the ultranationalists frequently cross this line to outright Islamophobia and a dislike of Muslims as people.

The rise of nationalist and far-right parties is anathema to the ideology of the EU, which sees itself as a union of liberal democracies. Now the nature of those democracies is under threat across the EU, not just in the eastern countries such as Hungary and Slovakia. In essence the divide is between those who are tolerant of intolerance and those who are not. Germany has played a central role in both the EU and the migrant crisis, so it is worth exploring the way in which events have unfolded there. It will be some time before the issues are resolved.

Angela Merkel opened Germany's doors to migrants and refugees in 2015. She was criticized by other EU leaders, certainly, but also started to face increasing opposition within Germany itself. This is not to say that Germany has been unwelcoming. The state has been working flat out to accommodate the newcomers, and thousands of ordinary people have volunteered to help in the refugee centers, as well as offering a wide range of services including language teaching and employment mentoring. Nevertheless, as more and more migrants have arrived, problems have emerged as people have started to grasp the scale of the task ahead in creating an integrated society. In 2015 alone, almost a million non-EU citizens arrived in Germany; most were Syrian, followed by Afghans, Iraqis, Iranians, and Eritreans. The Germans had not experienced the movement of peoples on such a scale since the end of World War II.

One of the initial problems is that new arrivals tend to gravitate to areas where ethnically similar communities have already been established, which can lead to problems with integration and can rapidly change the demographic and cultural character of districts. As the Federal Office for Migration and Refugees observed, "Refugees want to go to places where they are among themselves: Pakistanis want to go to the Rhine-Main area, Afghans move to Hamburg, Syrians to Berlin. But in dense areas, housing space is scarce and rents are high. Ghettos evolve quickly."

As the initial wave of public goodwill has subsided, fueled also by incidents such as the numerous sexual assaults in Cologne on New Year's Eve 2015, which were largely attributed to the immigrant population (although there were only a handful of convictions), Germany has seen a steady rise in violence against immigrants. In 2015 more than a thousand attacks were made on refugee shelters. That was at the height of the migrant crisis, but in 2016, when the number of people arriving had dropped significantly to under three hundred thousand as a result of the deal with Turkey to reduce the flow across the Aegean, a similar number of incidents still occurred.

In Germany the outlines of the Berlin Wall and the Iron Curtain can still be traced in matters more serious than food and accents, and this is especially true when it comes to immigration. Attitudes toward immigrants are much more negative once you cross the river Elbe eastward. Put simply, more immigrants are in western Germany than in its east (other than Berlin) due to a quota system used to distribute refugees and asylum seekers across the country; as the eastern states are poorer and less populated, they have received fewer of the new arrivals. In both 2015 and 2016, three of the western states, Bavaria, North Rhine-Westphalia, and Baden-Württemberg, took almost 50 percent of the migrants/refugees. By contrast, in 2015 Saxony-Anhalt received 2.8 percent, Mecklenburg-Vorpommern 2 percent, and Brandenburg 3.1 percent. But despite this, many more physical attacks on migrants occur in the east. Germany's domestic intelligence agency (BfV) produced a 2016 report stating that the western states averaged 10.5 extremist attacks per million people. In the eastern state of Saxony this rose to 49.6 attacks, in Brandenburg to 51.9, and in

Mecklenburg-Vorpommern to 58.7. The three regions are also home to the largest groups of organized neo-Nazis.

In 2016 the German government's annual report "Status of German Unity" noted not only the effects on those suffering discrimination, but also, according to Iris Gleicke from the Federal Ministry for Economic Affairs and Energy, that the difficulties of securing "social peace in eastern Germany" were causing a "very serious threat to the economic development" there. She also noted, "The large majority of eastern Germans are not xenophobic or right-wing extremists." Germans are careful with historical references, but the scale of the attacks led Gleicke to invoke the memory of the 1930s and Hitler's brownshirts: "We East Germans have to take the matter into our own hands and decide whether we want to protect our cities and villages or leave them to the brown nightmare. Society should not look away when people are attacked or refugee shelters are set on fire." Such comments resonate deeply in the German psyche, but a growing contingent of people do not want the country's past mistakes to dictate how they must feel, or what they can and can't say. Which brings us to the Patriotic Europeans Against the Islamisation of the West (PEGIDA) and the Alternative for Germany (AfD).

As early as 2014, members of PEGIDA were marching in Dresden and other Eastern cities. This overt hostility put it beyond mainstream politics, but by early 2015 it was attracting huge crowds and had spread across the country. One demonstration in Leipzig drew thirty thousand people, twenty thousand turned out in Munich, nineteen thousand in Hanover, and ten thousand in Dresden. As so often happens when politics moves from the fringe into wider society, many of the rallying cries heard at the demonstrations had first been voiced in the stands of football stadiums. A notable example was the Dynamo Dresden Ultras, fans who beat President Trump to the term *Lügenpresse* (lying press) by at least a year. From the Dresden stands the chant spread to the streets. The crowds felt that the authorities, in league with the media, were not telling them the truth about immigration.

By the early summer support for the party had dropped, due to a combination of "demonstration fatigue" and a series of scandals involving PEGIDA leaders, including a picture of the founder of the movement, Lutz Bachmann, posing as Hitler. But the underlying sentiments had not gone away, and as the migration crisis peaked that summer of 2015, they came back to the surface, creating the political space for a more "palatable" version of PEGIDA—the AfD.

The AfD had formed back in 2013, but its focus then was campaigning against the euro currency. As the migrant crisis began to grow, it turned its attention toward immigration and forged contacts with PEGIDA. By summer 2016, with PEGIDA floundering, AfD was well positioned to take over as the biggest radical right-wing movement. It quickly grew in both membership and representation in the state parliaments. The alarm bells began really sounding when it finished second in the Mecklenburg-Vorpommern election, taking 21 percent of the vote and leaving Chancellor Merkel's Christian Democractic Union of Germany (CDU) party in third place. By the time of the general election in late 2017, AfD was well organized and popular enough to enter the Bundestag in large numbers, winning almost a hundred seats. This was the first time the extreme Right had been represented there since the early 1960s. Although Angela Merkel's party gained the biggest share of the vote, the AfD made significant gains, particularly in the east of the country, coming in third overall in the election. The political center of gravity in Europe was again starkly divided.

AfD policies include the rejection of the Schengen Area and the creation of permanent border controls at both the national and the EU level. It supports enhanced vetting of asylum seekers and says Germany has no place for Muslim practices and beliefs if these run counter to "the free democratic social foundation, our laws, and the Judeo-Christian and humanistic bases of our culture," according to party paraphernalia. Softening its stance, it does accept that Muslims can be "valued members of society," but argues that multiculturalism does not work. It is also against the euro, campaigns for the deutsche mark to be reinstated, and wants powers returned to the nation-state.

All of these ideas are echoed right across the Continent. The regional and political rifts we see in Germany are opening up everywhere. In the Dutch general election of March 2017 the far-right Party for Freedom became the second-largest party. In May the National Front's Marine Le Pen went through to the second round of the French presidential election and won 33.9 percent of the vote, almost doubling the share of her father, Jean-Marie, in 2002. Austria's Freedom Party has also enjoyed increased support, coming in third in the election in October 2017. Even Chancellor Merkel tacked sharply to the right in the 2017 election campaign as she sought to close off the growth of the extreme Right. In liberal democracies, those who cannot crush domestic antidemocratic movements need to find ways to manage them.

As early as 2014 the stresses of migration prompted the Hungarian prime minister, Viktor Orbán, to say he wanted to create an "illiberal democracy." Behind this phrase is the idea that liberal policies and values can be rejected by an electorate that votes as part of a nationalist party hostile to these things, but the country remains a democracy. The Polish government elected in 2015 held similar views. This ideology runs counter to the ideals of the EU and is one of the growing divisions threatening to splinter the union. As the Brookings Institution states in a report on migration, "The crisis has destabilized the politics of the entire European continent, roiling the political systems of individual countries and threatening the solidarity of the EU as a whole."

This is a fundamental challenge to a divided Europe. It is not just about immigration; it is also about economies, trade, sovereignty, and liberalism in general. But, as we cope with the new realities of mass immigration and the moral necessity to take in refugees, we must not lose sight of core values. If we do, we may condemn all future Europeans, from whatever background, to live in a more repressive society than at present. It's worth remembering that most of those coming to Europe are trying to get away from despotic regimes that have failed them. We need to deal with radical Islamism, manage mass migration, and care for refugees, but in a manner that does not undermine our liberal values and rule-of-law-based systems.

Those laws, values, and that system are what eventually healed the most recent great schism in Europe, the one that developed after 1945. Now divisions, new and old, are again appearing. The next few years will show us if we can make a safe European home or will go backward into a divided future.

CHAPTER 8

UK

Each man is an island unto himself. But though a sea of difference may divide us, an entire world of commonality lies beneath.

—James Rozoff

Previous pages: Hadrian's Wall, Northumberland, a stone wall that was built to defend Roman-conquered Britain from the northern tribes.

I magine you're a Roman soldier posted to Hadrian's Wall, c. 380 CE. You're from the Etruria/Tuscany region, one of the relatively few soldiers serving in your legion who is actually from the Italian peninsula. It's February, freezing cold, and you're on the night shift looking out from the ramparts. You can't even see the stars as it's cloudy, drizzling, and dawn is approaching. A brisk wind is blowing up your tunic, and you're thanking Jupiter for the delivery of *braccae* (woolen trousers), which arrived last week and were only three months late. It's difficult to know which is worse, the weather or the sporadic attacks from the barbarians north of the wall. Your colleague on the night watch on your stretch of the wall isn't of much comfort as he's from northern Gaul, doesn't speak much Latin, and only joined up so that after twenty-five years of service he might get Roman citizenship.

You look out at the vague outlines of this barren land, its sparse grasses and rushes bent in the wind, you think of home, the towns of Lucca and Siena, the countryside, the coastline. You sigh heavily and say to yourself, "*Pro di immortales, quid hic facio?*" "What the hell am I doing *here?*" Or words to that effect.

Hadrian's Wall must have been quite a sight for the "primitive" island tribes. Built in 122 CE, it was seventy-three miles long, and parts of it were fifteen feet high and ten feet deep. A thirteen-foot-deep, thirty-foot-wide "fighting ditch" was dug in front of it. Between the two were thickets of spikes. The numerous gates were fortified, and at every Roman mile along the wall was a small fort, and between each of these two turrets. On one side of this wall was "civilization," on the other "barbarians." To this day some English and Scots joke that this is still the case, though the wall is no longer there to separate them.

Over fifteen hundred years, Hadrian's Wall, symbol of the great reach of the Roman Empire—as well as its limitations—almost disappeared. After the Romans left, it fell into disrepair. Farmers took bits of it to build houses and sheep pens, the burgeoning Christian communities took more for churches, and little by little, as the memory of the Romans in Britain faded, their wall crumbled into the landscape they had sought to conquer.

The Romans never succeeded in uniting the lands. Hadrian's Wall was built to defend the conquered territory against the parts they couldn't rule. When they'd first arrived in southeast England in 43 CE, they found an array of Iron Age tribes. These tribes knew of the Romans; they would already have had some cultural and economic interactions with the empire and would also have heard stories of Rome's military capabilities from Julius Caesar's incursions almost a century earlier. Back then the tribes had put up fierce resistance, but when the legions fell upon them this time they were unprepared, and crucially, they were not united. They were overrun by the Romans, who then set themselves up in Colchester as they prepared to occupy the whole island.

Historians believe that by 47 CE eleven tribes in the southeast had surrendered, and the Romans controlled the area from south of the Humber in what is now Hull across to the river Severn estuary near the Welsh border. From there, the arduous push into Wales and the north began. By 84 CE they were as far up as the Moray Firth, about 150 miles inside what is now Scotland. Evidence suggests that the Romans sailed up as far as the peninsula of Kintyre, and legionnaires probed into the Highlands, but the Moray Firth was the limit of their settled power in Britain. Had they been able to continue, put the whole island under single

rule, and remain, the history of the United Kingdom could have
been very different.

But the Roman Empire's borders were being threatened elsewhere, and troops were needed to defend the heartland, not push
forward on the fringes. Back the Romans came, stopping more
or less where the modern England-Scotland border is. And after
they stopped, they built their wall, the most important surviving
testament to the strength and reach of Rome's military prowess.
Geographically the region does not have the rivers, say, or mountains that so often form natural boundaries. But it was where the
Romans drew the line militarily.

The wall helped shape the place that would eventually be
known as the United Kingdom. For two and a half centuries the
line held. Below it, life grew increasingly Romanized; above it, a
different Celtic culture continued. The future Wales and Scotland were never fully defeated and would always retain a sense of
difference from the region that became known as England—the
part of Britannia where Pax Romana held sway and where most
of the Roman roads and towns were built.

By 211 CE southern England was called Britannia Superior
on the grounds that it was closer to Rome. The capital was moved
to London. Northern England was Britannia Inferior (another
distinction still relevant today), and York was declared its capital. By the year 296 the land had been further divided. Now the
south was called Britannia Prima, the north up to Hadrian's Wall
was Maxima Caesariensis, the Midlands were governed as Flavia
Caesariensis, and Wales was known as Britannia Secunda. None
of it would last in name, but the outlines of those demarcations
are still seen today.

Eventually, events on the Continent conspired against the
Romans. A couple years after our Roman soldier asked himself
his rhetorical question, General Magnus Maximus asked himself
the same thing, and in 383 CE his answer was to take his legions

home to challenge the emperor of Rome. A few years later, the entire apparatus of the empire's northernmost outpost packed up and headed for Rome.

After Maximus left, the "barbarians" (Picts and Scots) broke through to the south, prompting the Britons to petition Rome to send a legion to expel them, which it did. Hadrian's Wall had by then fallen into disrepair, so the Romans advised the British to build a frontier barrier to keep the northerners out. However, the Romans failed to provide the know-how to use stone, and the British put up a turf wall. The "barbarians" cut straight through, resulting in a second plea to Rome—the same as the first: "Save us!" Again the legion returned, beat back the invaders, and this time showed the locals how to construct a stone wall.

It was no good. Without the Romans, even stone could not hold back the hordes from the north. A third appeal was made—this one known as the Groans of the Britons. The response this time has gone down in the annals of British history and is to this day used in political discourse. Rome wrote back, "Look to your own defenses." The unifying power in Europe had rejected the British, the British had rejected the unifying power, and they were indeed on their own, looking to their "own defenses." Comparisons to Brexit are fun, but not necessarily germane. The problem then was that there weren't any defenses. The shadows were lengthening; the twilight of Roman Britain was giving way to the Dark Ages.

In the late 600s enough of Hadrian's Wall was still standing for the great Anglo-Saxon scholar the Venerable Bede to describe a section of the wall near the river Tyne as "eight feet wide and twelve high, in a straight line from east to west as is clear to beholders to this day." But it was already becoming a diminished structure. By the 1700s it meant so little to people that what appears to be one of the greatest acts of cultural vandalism in British history occurred.

In 1745 Field Marshal George Wade was tasked with intercepting the Jacobite army of Bonnie Prince Charlie as it headed south. His troops and artillery, marching west from Newcastle, failed due to the lack of a solid road. This prompted Wade to build a new, cross-country road to Carlisle, along the ancient route of Hadrian's Wall. He had a long history of road building in Scotland, and a reputation as a no-nonsense military man. The nearest building materials to hand were within his field of vision—it must have seemed obvious that the thing to do was to pull down large sections of the wall and use them as the bedrock of about thirty miles of his road.

The destruction of the wall continued until the 1800s, when its value as a great historic monument began to be more widely recognized. Conservationists took up the cause, and stretches of the wall were cleared of debris and foliage and maintained. The best-preserved sections are in a twenty-mile stretch in Northumberland between Hexham and Haltwhistle and are now one of the great tourist attractions of the UK. In the summer months thousands of keen walkers follow the trail across the same gloriously bleak countryside the Romans encountered all those centuries ago. In winter, though, you get a better feel of what was for them the outer edges of civilization. Most of the towers, crenellations, and gates may have gone, but the wall still stands, both physically and in the collective imagination of the British. It reminds them of the time when they were first politically connected to the mainland of the European continent, when the dividing line was drawn between the two largest constituencies of the island—England and Scotland.

Even now, in the twenty-first century, with much of the wall long gone, even though most of it actually lies south of the Scottish border, the Roman fortification still symbolizes one of the main divisions in what, paradoxically, remains a united kingdom.

Whereas in Europe we see the difficulty of getting nation-states, and the peoples they represent, to unify under one banner, the

United Kingdom has been uniting different peoples and identities for hundreds of years.

Right now, the UK is going through a real moment of "us and them," between the nations it comprises and within its populations, and many people feel more divided than ever. This has been exacerbated in recent years by the 2016 vote to leave the European Union and its aftermath. Cultures and identities are diverging, interacting in new ways with bigger issues of globalization, nationalism, and the EU.

The majority of Brits are bound together legally, linguistically, and to a great extent culturally. Scotland and England were distinct nations for much of their history, with an often fractious relationship. Much of the trouble started in the thirteenth century, when Edward I of England tried to claim Scotland. After many years of fighting against the English invaders, Scotland's independence was regained by Robert the Bruce in 1314. Over the subsequent centuries the border was often a hot spot, with raids and incursions from both sides, but the two countries were brought closer together in 1603 when James VI of Scotland also became James I of England, and finally they were officially joined together in the Acts of Union 1707.

Scotland may not be a separate nation-state, but the Scots are a nation quite distinct from the English—and, perhaps most important, they feel that way. The differences between them can be exaggerated, but they do exist, and not just because a greater proportion of men wear skirts north of the border.

Until a few centuries ago there was a mild ethnic difference. The Scots were descended from Celtic peoples, as were the Welsh and Cornish. They came to the islands about four thousand years ago and even inhabited what is now England, although there they were gradually replaced by Frisians, Angles, Jutes, and Saxons. Although the genetic differences between English and Scots are now barely noticeable, to this day the English are sometimes called *Sassenachs* by the Scots, which is Gaelic for "Saxons."

Gaelic, or *Gàidhlig*, was the first language for most people in northwest Scotland during the seventeenth century. But within fifty years of the Acts of Union, only about 23 percent of people spoke the language; this number had shrunk to 4.5 percent in 1901, and 1.2 percent at the turn of this century. About sixty thousand people now speak Gaelic, mostly in the Western Isles, and they are bilingual. The Scots are very aware that their current native tongue is not derived from their original language. What they are left with is historical memory—the knowledge that once they were very different. The English have a vague recollection of being the far larger and sometimes dominant force in the relationship; the Scottish have a much keener sense of oppression.

The question of self-determination has not gone away despite increased independence for Scotland within the Union. When England and Scotland were first joined together, Scotland retained control over its educational and legal systems—for example, English law allows for "guilty" or "not guilty," but Scottish law has a third category, "not proven." Leave to one side the joke that this sometimes translates as "Not guilty—and don't do it again"; it satisfies one of the fundamental tenets of self-rule: overseeing your own judicial system. But Scotland and England were largely ruled as one. Not until 1885 was the post of secretary for Scotland created, and even then it was a junior position. It finally became a senior cabinet post, with the title secretary of state for Scotland, in 1926.

In 1997 a referendum was held on proposals for devolution, in which a firm majority voted in favor. In 1998 the Scotland Act was introduced, creating a Scottish executive and Scottish parliament based in Edinburgh that had significant powers, devolved from London, in what were judged to be specifically Scottish affairs. In 2007 the executive rebranded itself the Scottish government, a term that gained legal recognition in 2012. The following year it called for an independence referendum in 2014. The breakup of the UK now looked like a distinct possibility. With just two days to go before voting, the three main British political parties, by now thoroughly rattled and hoping for a "no" vote, said that if independence was rejected, "extensive new powers" would be given to the Scottish parliament. This was probably one of the reasons for the final result: 55 percent voted against independence.

Following the referendum, Westminster went ahead with the 2016 Scotland Act, which gave Scotland's parliament control over a wider range of matters, including the ability to amend the Scotland Act of 1998, management of the British Transport Police in Scotland, the right to keep half of the VAT raised in Scotland, and decision making over speed limits and road signs. The latter two may seem relatively trivial compared to powers over education and law, but control of minor issues, as well as great affairs of state, satisfies the need for control of what are perceived as one's own affairs.

Perhaps this is the reason for the apparent decline in support for independence. Following the result, people were soon talking of a second referendum, and in the 2015 general election, a massive surge of support for the Scottish National Party (SNP) increased its number of seats in the House of Commons from six to fifty-six. However, since then, with the new powers coming through, people have seemed less interested, and the SNP's focus on a second referendum is perhaps the reason why it hemorrhaged support in the 2017 general election, losing twenty-one seats. It now seems that for the foreseeable future the kingdom will remain united. Scottish identity is strong, but not strong enough for the majority of the population to want it reflected in an independent state. The United Kingdom as a concept still supersedes the differences in identity that exist between the various nations it comprises.

Much of what has been said here about the Scottish-English relationship could be said about that between the Welsh and the English. Again, the English are less aware of the oppression for which their ancestors were responsible than are the Welsh, and this gives an occasional sharp edge to the relationship. But powers have now been devolved to a Welsh national parliament, which has gone a long way in answering questions about self-rule. The suppression of the Welsh language ended long ago: several acts of Parliament have guaranteed its equality in law with English, and Welsh-language TV and radio stations have been set up; this has encouraged a resurgence in its use. Roughly 20 percent of Welsh people speak Cymraeg—that's around half a million. A Celtic language, it's closely related to Cornish, and both can be traced back to the language spoken in those regions in the sixth century.

The Cornish also see themselves as a separate region from the rest of the country—Cornish nationalists say that England begins "east of the river Tamar," which divides Cornwall from Devon. The Cornish were officially recognized as a national minority group in 2014; nevertheless, support for Cornish independence has not yet spread beyond the fringes of politics.

While having a strong sense of their own identity, most people in the British Isles get along fine, subscribing to the same values and to the overarching idea of the Union. Of course, anti-English sentiment is expressed in both Wales and Scotland—I was once effectively refused service in a workingmen's club in Perthshire. However, such incidents are rare, and for every bigot, thousands of other people rarely give the differences a second thought except in usually well-intentioned banter or teasing.

As a young Englishman I was on a train along with several hundred Scotsmen going to Wrexham to see Scotland play Wales. The journey was one long drinking session punctuated with songs, the lyrics including "If you hate the fucking English, clap your hands." My hands may have hurt from enthusiastic clapping, but

I did not mistake the sentiments of some soccer fans for those of the entire Scottish nation. *Hate* is a word bandied about in the stands; away from the stadium, most people behave in a more grown-up manner. Just as many Brits who voted to leave the EU did not do so from chauvinistic, extreme nationalism, so many Scots who voted to leave the UK were not anti-English.

Most of the ancient British "tribes" live intermingled, working, living, and playing together. As the population of this relatively crowded island approaches 70 million, it is crucial that the cohesion remains—or, if one of the peoples does decide to break the legal ties, that it is done peacefully. In the past century, in only one corner of the kingdom has this not always been the case—Northern Ireland.

Northern Ireland is the smallest of the four main UK regions, representing just 5.7 percent of the land area and, with 1.8 million people, 2.9 percent of its population. It was created in 1921 after the British government divided Ireland into two separate jurisdictions. "Southern Ireland" became independent in 1922, while Northern Ireland remained part of the UK. Some people think that the terms *United Kingdom* and *Great Britain* are interchangeable, but the latter refers only to England, Scotland, and Wales (and a few small adjacent islands), whereas the UK also comprises Northern Ireland. The full title is The United Kingdom of Great Britain and Northern Ireland.

From the beginning, Northern Ireland's population was split between Protestants (the majority) and Catholics. The Protestants tended to be descendants of settlers from Scotland, and to a lesser extent England. Most were and are Unionists and want to stay in the UK; most Catholics were and are Nationalists, who want a united Ireland, although they disagree about how to achieve this. The animosity between the two communities has frequently erupted in violence, the worst of which came during the three decades of the Troubles, which began in the late 1960s and cost more than thirty-five hundred people their lives, with another fifty thousand injured.

The 1998 power-sharing Good Friday Agreement ended most of the violence and the resulting "peace dividend" has helped drive economic growth and a reduction in unemployment. Nevertheless, Northern Ireland remains deeply divided—with an entrenched culture of "us and them." Few elements of life are as bisected as education and housing, something that is obvious in the capital, Belfast, with physical walls built between the two sides. They are known, collectively, as the Peace Walls, but the sad irony is that they symbolize conflict. This is no continuous, imposing barrier such as that along the West Bank or the Saudi Arabia–Iraq border, but rather a series of somewhat ramshackle concrete and metal structures that zigzag through several of the poorer districts of Belfast, mostly in the north of the city. They started to appear at the beginning of the Troubles. Many begin and end seemingly without reason, but the locals know why: they mark the division of Protestant and Catholic territories between which, without the walls, violence might be more frequent.

Henry Robinson understands the width and depth of these divides better than most. A former member of the Official IRA, he was jailed in his youth for kneecapping a man from the rival Provisional IRA. However, having served a sentence in Crumlin Road Gaol, he has devoted his life to conflict resolution in Northern Ireland, as well as around the world in places such as Colombia. He believes the walls are standing in the way of reconciliation: "I call them Conflict Walls or Hate Walls. The conflict is over, but sectarianism has been allowed to continue to be embedded in society, and the evidence for that is the increase in the number of walls since the conflict ended."

In all, Belfast has about a hundred of these walls. They have even become something of a tourist attraction, and in the summer months you can see tourists arriving on buses from the cruise ships to gaze at them. They are a strange juxtaposition of the economic benefits that the peace dividend has brought alongside a reminder that the peace is fragile. On each side of the walls the neighborhoods are festooned with the symbols and messages of the antagonists. Look up from the pavement curbs, painted in the colors of the Irish or UK flags, and you will see walls sporting slogans such as THE BRITS HAVEN'T GONE—NOR HAVE WE in support of the Real IRA or ULSTER WILL ALWAYS REMAIN BRITISH—NO SURRENDER. The whole sides of some buildings are given over to murals honoring paramilitary groups such as the IRA and the Ulster Freedom Fighters. Henry is unimpressed with this tribal loyalty: "I think both communities have become comfortable with the terror touts and almost take a perverse, ghoulish pride in the continuation of these monuments of hate. That's a barometer that maybe things could go wrong in the future unless it's dealt with."

The division exists across Northern Ireland, with walls in other urban areas such as Londonderry/Derry, albeit to a lesser extent. In the smaller towns it's harder to spot the fault lines—but they are there. One housing complex will be predominantly Protestant, another Catholic. A town's river might be the boundary. It is easy to find districts where 90 percent of residents are either Unionists or Nationalists. In everyday life many people do interact, and the more middle-class areas have a greater diversity in housing; many people don't make a conscious choice not to integrate with their neighbors. But the political and religious structures built into society shape the way people function and ensure that they lead parallel but separate lives.

Finding ways of breaking down these self-perpetuating divisions is hard. Just as neighborhoods are split, especially in public housing, so are schools. A scheme to integrate the system has faltered, and recent research found that in almost half of Northern Ireland's schools 95 percent of pupils were of the same religion.

Another generation of children is set to grow up belonging to one or the other of the two main factions in an educational system described in 2010 by Peter Robinson, then first minister in Northern Ireland, as a "benign form of apartheid which is fundamentally damaging to our society." Henry Robinson agrees: "The walls are symbolic of the nonphysical walls and the division where the majority of people educate their kids in separate religious schools. There is a culture of separation in Northern Ireland and a policy of integration, which doesn't marry up. . . . There's not enough community support or focus on bridge building on both sides."

While efforts to end the rift seem to have hit an impasse, something could soon have an impact: changing demographics. After the partition of Ireland in 1921, Protestants outnumbered Catholics in Northern Ireland by two to one, a ratio that lasted until the early 1970s. Now, however, Protestants are no longer even a majority of the total population: according to the 2011 census they accounted for 41.6 percent (across various denominations), with Catholics at 40.8 percent. The religious aspect of the conflict, which has faded in recent decades with the decline in religious practice, has been replaced by a clash of cultural identities: whether a person is a Catholic or a Protestant indicates whether the person is a Unionist or a Nationalist. With birth rates and religious identification declining more quickly among Protestants than Catholics, the Catholics will likely become a majority, which will bring with it political implications and questions about Northern Ireland's position in the UK.

That position is already problematic following the Brexit vote. The Northern Ireland–Ireland frontier is the only land border in the UK; how should it now be handled? The people and businesses in the region are able to move and trade freely across the border. How this might change could have far-reaching consequences and risks upsetting the fragile peace as well as boosting support for the union of Northern Ireland and Ireland. The British government has said it has no plans to install border controls, but that raises a number of problems—potentially allowing an open route for both people and goods between the UK and the EU, one of the very things people who voted to leave wanted to control.

Brexit has exposed deep divisions throughout the UK. It has exacerbated the old ones—the majority in both Scotland and Northern Ireland voted to remain—but also exposed a variety of differences within the population.

One of the clearest demarcations in British society has always been class, and this remains the case today. It might be less clear-cut than in the past—a middle-class teacher may well earn less than a working-class plumber, a train engineer may earn more than someone in middle management—and social mobility and diversity are greater. However, most social-mobility studies find that men and women who attended private schools and then one of the Russell Group universities (the UK's twenty-four leading universities) still dominate the highest positions in the land in numbers way above their proportion of the population as a whole. The case can be made that these people are the most highly educated, and in many instances the best, people for their jobs; but it can also be argued that this system prevents the UK from finding and utilizing the best of its talents.

Only 7 percent of the UK population attended independent schools, but they dominate the highest levels in the judiciary, the armed services, the BBC, the major corporations, the civil service, and both major political parties. For example, 55 percent of the civil service's permanent secretaries are privately educated, as are 71 percent of the top judges. About half of the UK's newspaper columnists are privately educated. A 2014 Social Mobility and Child Poverty Commission report found that on the BBC's

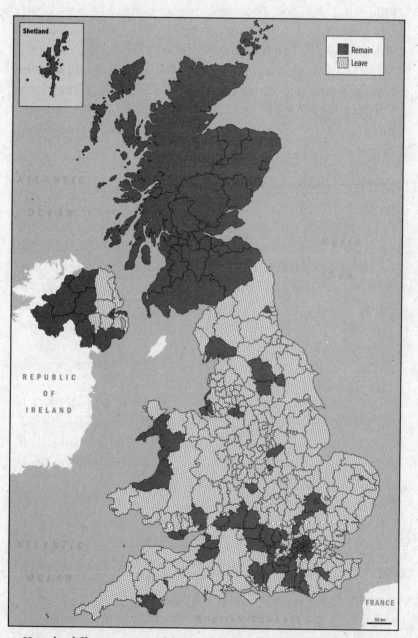

How the different regions of the UK voted in the 2016 EU referendum.

influential *Question Time* program, 43 percent of guests had attended Oxford or Cambridge Universities. Other factors are also at play that help perpetuate the imbalance across society. Many major companies offer only unpaid internships, effectively barring young people from applying unless their parents can subsidize their living costs. Consequently the better-off, many of them privately educated, gain the experience and contacts that help them succeed in the world of work.

With both politics and the media disproportionately packed with the privately educated, the latter tend to dominate public discourse, which can have a huge impact on influencing public opinion. But it can also mean that they represent a minority viewpoint, which runs the risk of obscuring how popular the opposing view really is, so that a large number of people become increasingly frustrated that their voices aren't being heard. That is partly what happened with Brexit, which is why in June 2016 the political, business, and media classes got the shock of their lives when the UK voted narrowly in favor of leaving the European Union. The less arrogant woke up and realized how out of touch they were with huge swathes of the electorate.

Since Brexit, much talk has been of the "left-behinds," which usually refers to those for whom EU membership and globalization have led not to a better life, but to competition for lower-skilled jobs and sometimes unemployment. Those who voted to leave the EU did so for many reasons and came from all walks of life, but certainly many were from the poorer regions of England and Wales, former working-class areas, reflecting the traditional class divide between rich and poor.

The old divisions are hard to overcome, and some commentators have also started to identify new rifts.

The writer David Goodhart characterized a major new difference in his 2017 book, *The Road to Somewhere*, "between the people who see the world from Anywhere and the people who see it from Somewhere." He argues, "Anywheres dominate our culture and society. They tend to do well at school and then usually move from home to a residential university in their late teens and on to a career in the professions that might take them to London or even abroad for a year or two." The Anywheres can feel at home wherever they go, whether that's Berlin, New York, Shanghai, or Mumbai. On the other hand the Somewheres tend to have a much more clearly defined sense of identity. Like the majority of people in Britain, they live within twenty miles of where they grew up and identify with locality, region, and country—they are more "rooted."

Among the Somewheres are many whose jobs have slowly disappeared as a result of the economic changes linked to globalization and whose working-class culture has recently been marginalized, especially in national discourse. The word *cosmopolitan* comes from Greek roots meaning "citizen of the world." We are indeed all one people, but to persuade those who live near where they grew up, have a strong local identity, and do not possess work skills that are transferable across continents that they are "cosmopolitan" is a challenge.

Goodhart suggests that up to 25 percent of the UK population are Anywheres, about 50 percent Somewheres, and the rest Inbetweeners. These are approximations and rough definitions, but they are useful in understanding modern Britain through the prism not just of class but of worldview. Many "progressive" Anywheres might be embarrassed about expressing love of country, Somewheres less so—their worldview was an accepted "fact" in British society until at least the late 1970s, but the rise of the multicultural society, parallel cultures, and the spread of higher education has challenged it.

Britain's Labour Party, the traditional party of the working class, is increasingly that of middle-class "progressives," many of whom lean toward the Anywheres' worldview. In the 1966 general election, Harold Wilson's Labour Party won power with approximately 11 million working-class votes and 2 million from the middle classes; in 2015 the figures for Labour stood at about 4.2 million working-class votes and 4.4 million middle-class ones. This changing pattern is down to a range of factors, not least the decline in traditional working-class jobs, but it is also because the party that traditionally concentrated on matters of vital importance to the working class—jobs, housing, and crime—has appeared to focus more on other issues, including identity politics.

These different identities—whether global or more rooted— have been in conflict with one another in debates about identity, nationalism, and, yes, immigration, before and after the Brexit vote. For decades this was in many ways a hidden discourse, as political and media circles seemed to refuse to engage with it. But nevertheless, huge numbers of the population were discussing it across the length and breadth of the land.

Successive governments backed mass immigration as needed for the current and future health of the economy of the UK. A strong case can be made for this. A glance at any of the big UK cities shows that transport, health, and many other industries would grind to a halt if all immigrants in the country simultaneously took the day off work. However, what was lacking was the concomitant funding of social housing and health care, and those in power tended to dismiss people's concerns without stopping to listen to them properly.

An example occurred in the UK general-election campaign of 2010. The then prime minister, Gordon Brown, had a televised street conversation with a lifelong working-class Labour voter, sixty-five-year-old Gillian Duffy, in the northern town of Rochdale. Mrs. Duffy ventured a range of views on the national debt, education, and the health service, then said, "You can't say anything about the immigrants because you're saying that you're . . . but all these Eastern Europeans what [sic] are coming in, where are they flocking from?" Her comments suggested she felt that if she expressed her uncertainty about the pace of change in her hometown, she would be considered a racist. Unwittingly, the prime minister confirmed her view. After joking with her, smiling, patting her on the back, and wishing her all the best, he got into his car. Then, forgetting that his microphone was still on, he said to an aide, "That was a disaster. Well, I just . . . should never have put me in with that woman. Whose idea was that?" Then, in response to an aide's asking what she'd said, Brown said, "Oh, everything, she was just a sort of bigoted woman." Millions of people in the UK who were also anxious about how their hometowns were changing realized that their prime minister thought they were bigots.

Many economists argue that the UK does indeed need immigration; the problem is that it has happened quickly, and the government didn't take into account the consequences when assessing projections for immigration after ten Eastern European countries joined the EU in 2004. The projections turned out to be far from realistic. A 2003 report for the Home Office claimed that as few as thirteen thousand people a year would come from countries such as Poland and Hungary, if Germany and other major EU countries kept their labor markets open as well. That turned out to be an important if. "Come on in," said the UK government; "Don't come on in," said most of the other EU countries—only three countries (the UK, Ireland, and Sweden) allowed Eastern Europeans immediate access to their labor markets in 2004. The rest of the member states introduced a variety of restrictions, with a view to a more gradual change over a number of years. By mid-2015 about nine hundred thousand people had arrived in the UK from Poland alone. In mid-2017, according to the UK's Office for National Statistics, between 2004 and 2016 net migration into the UK averaged 250,000 people a year. Combined, that is roughly the equivalent to the population of six cities each the size of Liverpool.

Given these statistics, it is unsurprising that in a 2011 YouGov poll 62 percent of respondents agreed, "Britain has changed in recent times beyond recognition; it sometimes feels like a foreign country and this makes me feel uncomfortable." Some people jump on such sentiments as proof of xenophobia and an irrational response to the benefits both of membership in the EU and of globalization. This is somewhat unfair to ordinary people who have seen their neighborhoods or the urban areas they visit undergo rapid change. Some areas have been transformed; that this can make some British feel uncomfortable is as obvious as saying that if large numbers of foreigners suddenly moved into a few districts of Ho Chi Minh City in Vietnam, the local people would feel uncomfortable.

It's ironic that the same person who decries middle-class gentrification of a working-class area, and who understands how the working class might not exactly embrace such change, is often quick to criticize people who are uneasy about the ways in which immigration can alter a neighborhood. Gentrification is sometimes even called *social cleansing*, while immigration is termed *diversification*. What is almost always true is that many of those using these terms are less affected by the changes than those living on the spot. To dismiss people who enjoyed their relatively homogeneous cultures and who are now unsure of their place in the world merely drives them into the arms of those who would exploit their anxieties—the real bigots.

Most British now accept the ideas of ethnic equality, gender equality, and gay marriage. Being anti-immigration does not necessarily accord with being anti-immigrant. Just as there is a difference between being uncomfortable about change and being racist, the same is true of patriotism and nationalism. I define the former partially as "love of one's own country and respect for those of others" and the latter as "love of one's own country and contempt for those of others." History has shown that it takes time for us to feel comfortable with "the other," but also that, properly managed, both We and They can learn to embrace each other.

This is just as true when it comes to the thorny issue of religion. The 2011 census counted dozens of religions in England and Wales, including Jedi Knights, Heavy Metal, and Satanism. However, these faiths, along with Christianity, Islam, and Hinduism, are practiced by a minority of the population of 65 million.

About two-thirds of the people have no participatory connection with a religion or place of worship, which shows what an anomaly Northern Ireland is—the strong religious identities there don't reflect the reality in the rest of the UK. Church attendance overall continues to decline year on year, a trajectory that began in the 1950s and has accelerated. Despite Christianity's precipitous decline, 59.3 percent of respondents in the 2011 census claimed to be Christians. This is clearly a cultural relic from times when almost the entire country professed to believe in Christianity and shows that even if many people don't accept the tenets of the faith, they identify culturally with its history and traditions. But this too is fading: in the 2001 census 72 percent had identified as Christian.

In addition to the 59.3 percent figure for Christians, the 2011 census found that 4.8 percent identified as Muslims, 1.5 percent as Hindus, 0.8 percent as Sikhs, and 0.5 percent as Jews. That correlates roughly as 2.7 million Muslims, 800,000 Hindus, 423,000 Sikhs, and 263,000 Jews. Along with "no religion," these are the top six categories in numbers. The Jedi Knights were seventh with 176,000 adherents—or possibly people with a particular sense of humor. Only 1,800 were self-declared Satanists.

The future increase in Jedi Knights, and indeed believers in Beelzebub, may be difficult to forecast, but this is less true of the main religions. The fastest-growing faith in the UK is Islam, partially because of birth rates, immigration, and devotion. Whereas most Britons who identify as being of Christian heritage are not religious—less than 7 percent of the population class themselves as practicing Christians—a 2014 poll found that 93 percent of Muslims said they practiced their religion. How much of this is devoutness and how much cultural pressure is difficult to judge, as in most Muslim cultures it is not acceptable to declare a "belief" in atheism. Given the strength of its following, and that one in three UK Muslims is under the age of fifteen, the rise of Islam as Britain's second-biggest declared religion seems likely to continue. And with ongoing immigration and the decline in church attendance in the Christian community, Islam will probably become the most practiced religion in the country.

That is a different thing, though, from the actual size of the Muslim population. In 2011 about one in twenty people in the UK were Muslim, but the public perception of the ratio is very different, as it is throughout Europe. An Ipsos MORI poll suggested that most Britons overestimate the number of Muslims by a factor of three. This is true of both the non-Muslim and the Muslim populations and may in part be due to the concentration of Muslims in urban areas—80 percent of Muslims live in just four regions: Yorkshire, the northwest, the West Midlands, and Greater London.

This concentration has given rise to the emergence of parallel societies, which can lead to division and challenge social cohesion. Parts of some urban areas (Luton, Burnley, Manchester, and Oldham, for example) are overwhelmingly Muslim and have little contact with nearby predominantly non-Muslim neighborhoods. Multiculturalism has not helped—it prevents assimilation and undermines social cohesion; we risk becoming many societies with different cultures, with reinforced "us and them" mentalities and lifestyles.

In the postwar years the UK struggled to become accustomed to being, in some regions, a multicultural society. The British are now engaged in a similar adjustment in an age of accelerated mass migration, but one that includes a significant additional factor, religion, which, as we've seen in Northern Ireland, can be one of the most difficult rifts to heal. As most faiths argue that theirs is the true way, and that others are at best misguided, faiths tend to separate people—an unwelcome development that some religious leaders actively encourage. This is particularly the case with Islam because, compared to other religions, Muslim groups are more politically involved, with a concomitant degree of media attention. Numerous religious women and men of different faiths are endeavoring to bridge the gaps, but too many mosques retain preachers who promote "us and them"—and many on the right wing of British politics are guilty of promoting the same thing.

The UK has long had an Islamic presence—a 1641 document refers to a "sect of Mahomatens," and the first translation of the Koran in England appeared in 1649. However, fifty years ago the estimated Muslim population was fifty thousand; now it is approaching 3 million. This is a rapid increase that occurred together with rapid changes in social attitudes in the UK. Christian church attendance declined, belief was eroded, and yet religious freedoms were increasingly accepted. Abortion became legal, as did the act of homosexuality. Gay marriage and the adoption of children by gay people is now routine, and the majority of the population, regardless of what some Christians say, accept most of the changes.

Tension comes with the growth of a religion many of whose adherents and leaders do not accept the above examples of modern liberal life as they go against the basic tenets of their faith. A poll conducted by ICM Research in 2016 found that 52 percent of British Muslim respondents believed that English law should be changed to make homosexuality illegal again. This attitude is not a problem when its adherents are so few that they have no power to change the status quo. For example, Britain's tiny ultraorthodox Jewish Hasidic population tends not to engage in the culture wars of the majority population and is content to pursue its own agenda within its own community. However, Islam is now and will increasingly be in a position to make its views known and heeded, which could have a major impact on society depending on what type of Islam it is—one that is pluralistic and in tune with the majority culture, or one that seeks to reverse the liberal changes for everyone, or one that insists on different laws for different people.

Will there be a Europeanization of Islam, or an Islamification of swathes of European urban areas? At the moment there are examples of both. Millions of modern Europeans are Muslim and fully participate in and are part of the fabric of whichever European country they are citizens of. But in some overwhelmingly Muslim urban areas Islamist ideology (often violent) is propagated by people seeking to control the residents. The more the latter is allowed to spread, the more difficult it will be for the former to resist it.

The answer to "What has my religion got to do with you?" is that we are all British and as such enjoy the right to hold and expound views as to what sort of society we want. The moment religion bumps up against the political arena of man-made laws, we all get a say: any Christian owner of a bed-and-breakfast business who tries to ban homosexuals will soon find this out. Those who claim to support the relatively progressive society that has been created must express confidence in the legitimacy of that progress in order to continue to enjoy the fruits of previous generations' political labors. This confidence appears to have been waning for many years now with the rise of "cultural relevancy," and a paralyzing fear that any criticism of aspects of a different culture will be branded racist. Naturally some people are clever enough to have spotted this anxiety and used it to close down debate. *Racism* is an increasingly easy, shallow term to throw around and in many cases deflects from our understanding of what is actually going in our society.

At its root this fear appears to derive from an overwhelming embarrassment, perhaps guilt, about the myriad evils of colonialism. Hence it might be troubling to fly the British flag, but to hoist that of a former British colony at a cultural event in the UK would be a legitimate expression of pride in culture. One type of patriotism, bad—another, good. This attitude is an interesting mix of guilt, paternalism, and authoritarianism. Many ordinary people in the UK are baffled by these cultural cringes because they do not inhabit the intellectual hinterland of those who propagate the dominant narrative. George Orwell was aware of all this. In the early 1940s he wrote in his essay "The Lion and the Unicorn":

> England is perhaps the only great country whose intellectuals are ashamed of their own nationality. In left-wing circles it is always felt that there is something slightly disgraceful in being an Englishman and that it is a duty to snigger at every English institution, from horse racing to suet puddings. It is a strange fact, but it is unquestionably true that almost any English intellectual would feel more ashamed of standing to attention during "God Save the King" than of stealing from a poor box.

Orwell was referring specifically to England, and perhaps his observations provide a clue to the rationale of some English pro-Brexit voters—those who do have a strong sense of national identity and pride and are bewildered by a political and media class seemingly detached from ordinary people's lives. Orwell was part of the commentariat before the expression was invented. He was an unusual example then for the same reasons as he would be now—he bothered to experience English culture as it is lived by large numbers of people. It taught him to try to understand better.

The UK has held together in the past in the face of nationalist sentiments and class and religious rifts. It is again being tested—whether it is able once more to overcome those divides and re-create the relatively cohesive societies of the twentieth century is yet to be seen. Hadrian's Wall shows us how far back our divisions go, and the Belfast walls how far we still have to go and how badly things can go wrong.

It is possible to look at the rifts in modern British society, and the competing narratives, and realize how important it is to balance the reasonable concerns of the different factions. Whether in England, Northern Ireland, Scotland, or Wales, communities need to be bound together in shared experience, cumulatively composing the nation-state—bound together, up to a point, with shared values, hard as they are to define. Our worst nightmare is a future in which we retreat into our various enclaves—the sum of the parts not equaling, but weakening, the whole.

Conclusion

The thing that hath been, it is that which shall be;
and that which is done, is that which shall be done;
and there is no new thing under the sun.

—Ecclesiastes 1:9

When working as a reporter, I once walked out of the Green
Zone in Baghdad with two colleagues at the height of the
bombing and kidnapping campaign in the early 2000s. The modus
operandi outside the Green Zone was to travel lying down on the
back seat of a beat-up car with tinted windows, accompanied by
two men with assault rifles up front. As I passed the last checkpoint guarded by American soldiers, every footstep began to take
on significance. With each one I was one step farther away from
safety—and assistance, should anything go wrong.

It is a strange space, one with few people and no one in charge.
There is no structure, no law, and the people who do venture into
this no-man's-land fall emphatically into "us" or "them" categories. Journalists used to be recognized as neutral, but those days
are mostly gone, and in many conflicts we are seen as targets
for retribution, or as cash cows to be sold or ransomed. On this
occasion we went a few hundred yards, spoke to a group of civilians, grew increasingly nervous, and hurried back to the relative
safety of the Green Zone, which was regularly mortared. But we
all agreed it was better to lose your head quickly to shrapnel than

to Abu Musab al-Zarqawi's knife-wielding gang—the embryonic "al-Qaeda in Iraq."

These strange places—the spaces in between—are often created by our conflicts and divisions. Sometimes they're still contested territory; sometimes they're mutually agreed buffer zones. Whichever they are, stepping into them can be unnerving. You do so at your own peril, often very aware that each side is training weapons on you as you proceed.

There are, alas, many modern examples. Cyprus is divided in half, between Greek and Turkish Cypriots, by a 111-mile-long buffer zone. The starkest part is the Varosha area of the city of Famagusta. In 1974 the inhabitants fled, fearing a massacre by Turkish troops, and never returned. Varosha is now sealed off by barbed wire, guard towers, and the Turkish military. Inside this ghost town it is mostly quiet, apart from birdsong. The streets are empty, the pavements overgrown with weeds, and many of the abandoned buildings are still in ruins from the war. At night the city disappears into the darkness, with no lights because there are no people. You cannot cross the Cypriot divide in Varosha, although now at seven points on the island an official from one side will check your passport before you go a few hundred yards until you reach the other side, whereupon you must present it again. Both sides watch the space in between, a shadowy place, beyond the confines of safety and comfort, where you are watched, and beyond which lies "the other."

Enforced separation and violent confrontations are the extreme effects of what happens when we build walls—and when the divisions they represent are apparently insurmountable. No one wants this; such spaces and such situations are frightening and dehumanizing. Going from one side to the other under scrutiny and threat can be unsettling.

Moving between Israel and Gaza is a cold, isolating experience: you feel as if you're caught somewhere between a sci-fi nightmare and some sort of lab experiment. To cross from Israel, you must pass through two Israeli checkpoints. Armed guards watch from behind bulletproof glass. Your belongings are thoroughly inspected. At the end of a long corridor you press a buzzer; the camera above takes a long look at you before the door clicks open. Now outside, you are in Gaza. But no people are here; you are in a fenced-off corridor, in a stretch of no-man's-land over a thousand yards wide (wider in some places). At last you emerge fully into the harsh sunlight and scrubland. Several hundred yards farther a Palestinian checkpoint awaits, where the inspections are less thorough. The return journey has much more stringent checks on the Israeli side: border guards monitor the banks of cameras from behind tinted windows; sound and touch sensors are fitted all along and near the wall; full-body scanners, the sort you find at airports now, are in use; luggage is swabbed for traces of explosives.

This may seem an unfriendly or overly rigorous routine, but arguably it works. The wall reduces the chances of suicide bombers from Gaza entering Israel, and the section of no-man's-land increases the range for rockets fired into Israel by at least a thousand yards. This is an uncomfortable truth. Yes, the sight of the Gaza wall, the barriers around Bangladesh, the barbed wire between Hungary and Serbia, offends our sensibilities and is testament to our failure to resolve our differences. It is easy to decry the trend of wall building; and walls can indeed imbue tough issues with a false sense of resolution. However, they can also provide temporary and partial alleviation of problems, even as countries work toward more lasting solutions, especially in areas of conflict. The Gaza wall, along with many other measures, for example the Iron Dome antimissile system, has dramatically reduced the number of fatalities on the Israeli side of that conflict. The Saudi wall with Iraq has helped prevent infiltration by IS.

But what of those walls in nonconflict areas? The barbed-wire policy of Hungary, in both the physical and the political sense, has reduced the inward flow of people, but is unlikely to stop it altogether. And mass migration isn't going to end in the foreseeable future. People on the move are fleeing poverty and/or violence, heading toward wealthier, more stable countries. While such levels of poverty and conflict prevail—and across the Middle East and Africa, that is likely to continue—the waves of migrants will keep coming, perhaps even increase. The world's population is still growing: in Africa, already home to widespread poverty, the population is expected to double, from 1.2 billion now to 2.4 billion within about thirty years. So although the poverty rate is decreasing, as the population increases, more people are likely to be trapped in poverty overall, with little hope or opportunity to change their circumstances.

A number of richer countries will continue to erect walls to help stem the flow of migrants. Some people argue, however, that we should simply dispense not just with walls, but with borders themselves—and allow completely free movement, so that any person can go anywhere on the planet he or she wishes.

In a 2017 *Foreign Affairs* essay, Nathan Smith, assistant professor of economics at Fresno Pacific University's School of Business, described this "open borders" idea as

> a regime of nearly complete freedom of migration worldwide, with rare exceptions for preventing terrorism or the spread of contagious disease. . . . Ending migration controls in this way would increase liberty, reduce global poverty, and accelerate economic growth. But more fundamentally, it would challenge the right of governments to regulate migration on the arbitrary grounds of sovereignty. . . . The more efficient allocation of labor would result in global increases in productivity, leading the world economy to nearly double in size. This increased economic activity would, moreover, disproportionately benefit the world's poorest people.

Smith argues that we could end world poverty by opening borders, and therefore we in the West have a moral duty to do so, especially as a means for righting historical wrongs. Some view the practice of citizenship within a state as being as violent and discriminatory as the slave trade because it places citizens' rights over human ones, legitimizing some people as more human than others. If borders were opened, the strain on resources in the West would be immense; welfare-state systems, for example, would have to be dismantled. Smith recognizes that "open borders would probably lead to a large increase in visible extreme poverty in the West," but counters that "impoverishment by Western standards looks like affluence to much of the world," and that the benefits to millions outweigh the inconveniences and downsides for Westerners.

At first glance this argument has logic. You can make the humanitarian case that, overall, things would level out. However, it doesn't appear to factor in two crucial elements. First, what effect would such mass movement have on the countries being abandoned? The initial emigrants would be those who could afford it, no longer having to make perilous journeys at the mercy of people traffickers and across deserts and seas. With fewer doctors, teachers, and other educated people, those abandoned countries would decline—perhaps even collapse and become utterly impoverished—with no prospect whatsoever of advancement.

The second problem is human nature—or, more specifically, group identity. An optimistic view maintains that the nation-states on the receiving end will struggle but cope, that they will absorb the newcomers. But a glance at history, and at the present, suggests a more cautious view of humanity may be required. Mass movements of people have already triggered the rise of nationalism: local populations do not seem to be happy when large numbers of outsiders descend upon them. The impact on politics in Europe is

clear: the Continent has moved sharply to the right and extreme
right. It is a similar story across the globe. It's commonplace to
read articles denouncing the Western countries for having some of
the most restrictive immigration laws and highest levels of racism
in the world. Elsewhere, they know better: other regions are just
as capable of being anti-immigrant, violent, religiously intolerant,
and racist. The pressures of globalization and rising population
numbers are being felt the world over, and we're seeing a rise in
nationalisms—both secular and religious—as a result. In India,
for example, given the prevalent attitude to the current levels of
immigration into the northeastern states, it seems unlikely that a
massive increase in migration from Bangladesh would reduce fric-
tion. Elsewhere, since 2014 the residents of the Paraguayan town
of Encarnación have been divided from their Argentine neighbors
in Posadas by a fifteen-foot-high, mile-long concrete wall along
the Paraná River on the Argentine side. Official reasons for the
construction were vague, but the context was clear: it was part of
increasing anxiety, in one of South America's most liberal countries,
over migration. Next to Paraguay is Bolivia, from where migration
into Argentina also comes. This prompted the congressman from
the northern Argentine province of Salta, Alfredo Olmedo, to say,
"We have to build a wall. . . . I agree 100 percent with Trump."

Open borders are not going to work in the current climate—
or even for the foreseeable future. The idea of the nation-state
has caused its share of problems, of course. We seem to have
recognized this when drawing up the UN laws on the ownership
of space, which state that

> outer space, including the Moon and other celestial bodies, is
> not subject to national appropriation by claim of sovereignty, by
> means of use or occupation, or by any other means. The Treaty
> establishes the exploration and use of outer space as the "province
> of all mankind." The Moon Agreement expands on these provi-

sions by stating that neither the surface nor the subsurface of the Moon (or other celestial bodies in the solar system), nor any part thereof or natural resources in place, shall become property of any State, international intergovernmental or non-governmental organization, national organization or non-governmental entity or of any natural person.

For the earth, however, it is too late to start again. The planet and its human inhabitants are too complex for a sudden shift to a global government in which nation-states are dissolved and the world is "the province of all mankind." The demise of the nation-state is frequently forecast for a variety of reasons: globalization, federal superstructures such as the EU, the rise of city-states, and, most recently, the rise of cryptocurrencies such as Bitcoin. And yet the nations and the states keep surviving. What's more, the world of nation-states that we live in has, for all its flaws, brought with it relative stability. We have come a long way, even if there is further to go. Measure the post–World War II era against the seventy-five years prior to it and you can see how much progress we've made. Globally, literacy rates are up, and poverty rates down. Diseases have been cured, infant mortality has been reduced, as has maternal death in childbirth. By means of science, democratic principles, and good leadership, this progress can continue.

However, if we do not move more money to where most people are, many of them will try to move to where the money is. In the immediate future foreign-aid budgets should be increased. In the near future, we need a twenty-first century Marshall Plan for the developing world to harness the riches of the G20 group of nations in a global redistribution of wealth. After the destruction of World War II, the Marshall Plan rebuilt Europe. This massive effort was driven by the Americans and carried out in the knowledge that it would benefit both sides. We now need a plan of even greater scope and ambition, executed in the knowledge

THE AGE OF WALLS

that it will benefit everyone. It should encompass development, infrastructure, trade, education, health, and climate change.

We have already had a taste of what will happen without such measures. Migration will continue, indeed grow, and in the face of this "threat" to their prosperity and stability, wealthier nations will only become more protective of what is theirs—territory, services, culture—further fueling nationalist movements and the fashion for wall building. Politics will become nastier, the barriers will be built higher, and increasingly violent attempts will be made to physically beat back those coming over the walls. Many hard-liners and xenophobes (often the same people) want zero immigration. This is undesirable from both a humanitarian and an economic standpoint.

The Western countries require immigrants for the midterm future to sustain themselves. I say *midterm* because I've yet to see a prediction of what will happen when the tipping point is reached—when technology, replacing most jobs, meets peak migration. But for now the world needs migration at sustainable levels that, for example, do not empty Bangladesh while destabilizing India. But how to control it is not clear: Who should be allowed in—economic migrants beneficial to a country's prosperity, or refugees fleeing war and persecution? Who decides who falls into the former category? How many should be permitted to come?

And how can these newcomers be integrated in a way that doesn't cause problems with the locals? Most of the West has accepted, and in some cases embraced, diversity. Any ideas of racial purity are long gone, confined to the fringe, such as we saw in the white supremacist demonstrations in Charlottesville, Virginia, in 2017. Any level of violence toward "the other" is unacceptable; the firebombing of migrant centers in Germany, for example, is a disgrace.

But while most Westerners don't engage in this sort of extreme behavior, they do want to preserve the underlying values of their

CONCLUSION   255

culture. After centuries of bloodshed, imperialism, and many other ills, the Western countries are now underpinned by a shared belief in democracy, gender equality, freedom of religion, and freedom of speech. Naturally, sometimes a nation does not conduct itself in accordance with its own civilized values, but this hypocrisy does not mean that the values are not there. What the majority of people want is for those coming to their communities to share their values, or at the very least to tolerate and not militate against them. A large proportion of modern Europeans would not object if a homosexual couple moved in next door, but they would be unhappy with a homophobic neighbor seeking to whip up hatred against homosexuals. So we need to find a way for newcomers to join the host community, not seek to undermine its values. This is not a question of race or religion, or simply good manners: the only place the guest gets to smash the plates is at a Greek restaurant. In this two-way relationship, it is also the host's responsibility to make the guest welcome. This applies to guests and hosts in countries and cultures the world over. Both sides can build bridges and reach across to "the other."

Until the universal brotherhood of man is accepted, and the world has no competition for resources, we will build walls. It was ever thus. We are animals. Wonderful, sometimes beautiful, sometimes ugly, incredible in our capability, infinite in our imagination, but still creatures of this world, and like every other creature we need our space.

A proverb found in most languages is "Good fences make good neighbors." This is not some trite folksy saying; it states an inevitable truth about boundaries both physical and psychological. We plan for a future in which we hope for the best and fear the worst, and because we fear, we build walls.

If that seems a deterministic view of humanity, there is an

upside. Our ability to think, and to build, also gives us the capacity to fill the spaces in between the walls with hope—to build bridges. For every wall between countries, there is an information superhighway; for every al-Qaeda, there is an interfaith outreach group; and for every missile-defense system, there is an international space station. Billions of dollars are donated in aid by rich nations. The codification of human rights acknowledges that, in theory, humans are all created equal. We have built great halls in which to meet, discuss, and try to resolve our differences. The United Nations, the EU, the African Union, ASEAN, Mercosur, OPEC, NATO, the World Bank, and hundreds of other pan-national and global organizations have all been created to help unite us and mediate our conflicts. They are a formal recognition of the human condition, and through them the megatribes seek to resolve their differences, maintaining their walls while searching for more lasting solutions.

So, although at present nationalism and identity politics are once again on the rise, the arc of history has the potential to bend back toward unity.

Acknowledgments

Thanks to all at Elliott & Thompson for constant support on a two-year project and for cutting enough "flowery stuff" to open a floristry. Thanks also to Wen Qi, Sabrina Zeng, Sam Bamba, Sameer Bazbaz, Mina al-Oraibi, Dr. Rogier Creemers, Dr. Reece Jones, Fawaz Gerges, David Waywell, Henry Robinson, Professor Stuart Elden, and David Kornbluth.

Bibliography

CHAPTER 1: CHINA

Bandurski, David. "China's 'positive' prescription for dissent." China Media Project, November 17, 2014. cmp.hku.hk/2014/11/17/37177/.

ChinaKnowledge.de. www.chinaknowledge.de/Literature/Historiog raphy/shiji.html.

"China's urban-rural divide." *OECD Observer*, October 2016. oec dobserver.org/news/fullstory.php/aid/5669/China_92s_urban -rural_divide.html#sthash.4EDnGCMf.dpuf.

Clapp, Frederick G. "Along and across the Great Wall of China." *Geographical Review* 9 (April–June 1920): 221–49.

Denyer, Simon. "China's scary lesson to the world: Censoring the internet works." *Washington Post*, May 23, 2016.

Goh, Chor-ching, Xubei Luo, and Nong Zhu. "Income growth, inequality and poverty reduction: A case study of eight provinces in China." *China Economic Review* 20, no. 3 (September 2009): 485–96.

Man, John. *The Great Wall*. London: Bantam Press, 2008.

Piketty, Thomas, and Gabriel Zucman. "Capital is back: Wealth-income ratios in rich countries, 1700–2010." *Quarterly Journal of Economics* 129, no. 3 (2014): 1255–1310.

Waldron, Arthur N. "The problem of the Great Wall of China." *Harvard Journal of Asiatic Studies* 43, no. 2 (December 1983): 643–63.

Whiteley, Patrick. "The era of prosperity is upon us." *China Daily*, October 19, 2007.

Wong, Sue-Lin, and Michael Martina. "China adopts cyber security law in face of overseas opposition." Reuters, November 7, 2016.

CHAPTER 2: USA

Channick, Robert. "Illinois contractor bidding to build Trump's border wall—with a tourist draw." *Chicago Tribune*, April 3, 2017.

Cook, Lindsey. "US education: Still separate and unequal." *US News*, January 28, 2015.

Dear, Michael. *Why Walls Won't Work: Repairing the US-Mexico Divide*. New York: Oxford University Press, 2015.

"Education at a glance 2012: OECD indicators." OECD Publishing, September 2012. www.oecd.org/edu/EAG%202012_e-book _EN_200912.pdf.

Goodhart, David. *The Road to Somewhere*. London: Hurst Publishers, 2017.

Hershbein, Brad. "A college degree is worth less if you are raised poor." Brookings Institution, February 19, 2016.

Martinez, Oscar J. "Border conflict, border fences, and the 'Tortilla Curtain' incident of 1978–1979." *Journal of the Southwest* 50, no. 3, "Fences" (Autumn 2008): 263–78.

Mexico's Constitution of 1917 with Amendments through 2015. Constitute. www.constituteproject.org/constitution/Mexico_2015 .pdf?lang=en.

Neeley, Jenny. "Over the line: Homeland Security's unconstitutional authority to waive all legal requirements for the purpose of building border infrastructure." *Arizona Journal of Environmental Law & Policy*, May 11, 2011.

Nowrasteh, Alex. "Guide to Trump's executive order to limit migration for 'national security' reasons." Washington, DC: Cato Institute, January 26, 2017.

Obama, Barack. "Floor statement on immigration reform" (speech). April 3, 2006. obamaspeeches.com/061-Immigration-Re form-Obama-Speech.htm.

"Political polarization in the American public." Pew Research Center, June 12, 2014. www.people-press.org/2014/06/12/political-polariza tion-in-the-american-public/.

Stovall, Preston. "Reassessing cultural divisions in the United States."
    Quillette, January 13, 2017.
Yearbook of Immigration Statistics. Washington, DC: DHS Office of
    Immigration Statistics, 2015.

CHAPTER 3: ISRAEL AND PALESTINE

"Behind the headlines: Facts and figures—Islam in Israel." Israel Min-
    istry of Foreign Affairs, June 9, 2016. mfa.gov.il/MFA/ForeignPolicy
    /Issues/Pages/Facts-and-Figures-Islam-in-Israel.aspx.
"A document of general principles and policies." Hamas, May 1, 2017.
    hamas.ps/en/post/678/a-document-of-general-principles-and
    -policies.
"Internal fight: Palestinian abuses in Gaza and the West Bank." Human
    Rights Watch, July 2009. www.hrw.org/report/2008/07/29/inter
    nal-fight/palestinian-abuses-gaza-and-west-bank.
"OECD reviews of labour market and social policies: Israel." OECD,
    January 2010. www.oecd-ilibrary.org/employment/oecd-reviews-of
    -labour-market-and-social-policies_20743408.
Starr, Kelsey Jo, and David Masci. "In Israel, Jews are united by home-
    land but divided into very different groups." Pew Research Center,
    March 8, 2016.
Vallet, Elisabeth, ed. *Borders, Fences and Walls: State of Insecurity?*
    Farnham, UK: Ashgate Publishing, 2014.

CHAPTER 4: THE MIDDLE EAST

Al Homayed, Tariq. "Interview with His Majesty King Abdullah II."
    Asharq Al-Awsat, January 23, 2007. kingabdullah.jo/en/interviews
    /interview-his-majesty-king-abdullah-ii-71.
"The Berm." GlobalSecurity.org. Accessed December 4, 2017. www
    .globalsecurity.org/military/world/gulf/kuwait-the-berm.htm.
Tomkins, Richard. "Airbus, Saudi Arabia finish Northern Border Security
    project." United Press International, September 23, 2014.

CHAPTER 5: THE INDIAN SUBCONTINENT

Ambedkar, B. R., and S. Anand. *Annihilation of Caste: The Annotated Critical Edition*. London and New York: Verso, 2014.

Coyderé, Hanne. "India: Violence against Dalits on the rise." *Diplomat*, May 19, 2016.

Hanson, S., R. Nicholls, N. Ranger, et al. "A global ranking of port cities with high exposure to climate extremes." *Climatic Change* 104, no. 1 (January 2011): 89–111.

Hasnain, Lieutenant General Syed Ata. "Why the fence on the line of control." *South Asia Defence and Strategic Review*, May 2014.

Jones, Reece. *Violent Borders: Refugees and the Right to Move*. London and New York: Verso, 2016.

Lindley Mark. "Changes in Mahatma Gandhi's views on caste and intermarriage." *Hacettepe University Social Sciences Journal* (Ankara, Turkey) 1 (1999).

Roy, Arundhati. "India's shame." *Prospect*, November 13, 2014.

Shamshad, Rizwana. "Politics and origin of the India-Bangladesh border fence." Paper presented to the 17th Biennial Conference of the Asian Studies Association of Australia in Melbourne, July 1–3, 2008.

"Skin colour tied to caste system, says study." *Times of India*, November 21, 2016.

Sukumaran Nair, P. *Indo-Bangladesh Relations*. New Delhi: APH Publishing, 2008.

Tripathi, Sanjeev. "Illegal immigration from Bangladesh to India: Toward a comprehensive solution." Carnegie India, June 29, 2016.

CHAPTER 6: AFRICA

Agyemang, Felix. "The emergence of gated communities in Ghana and their implications on urban planning and management." *Developing Country Studies* 3, no. 14 (July 2013): 40–46.

Aisien, Ebiuwa, and Felix O. U. Oriakhi. "Great Benin on the world stage: Reassessing Portugal-Benin diplomacy in the 15th and 16th centuries." *IOSR Journal of Humanities and Social Science* 11, no. 1 (May–June 2013): 107–15.

Beegle, Kathleen G., Luc Christiaensen, Andrew L. Dabalen, and Isis Gaddis. *Poverty in a Rising Africa: Overview.* Washington, DC: World Bank Group, 2015.

Breetzke, Gregory D., Karina Landman, and Ellen G. Cohn. "Is it safer behind the gates? Crime and gated communities in South Africa." *Journal of Housing and the Built Environment* 29, no. 1 (March 2014): 123–39.

Ediagbonya, Michael. "A study of the Portuguese-Benin trade relations: Ughoton as a Benin port (1485–1506)." *International Journal of Humanities and Cultural Studies* 2, no. 2 (July–September 2015): 206–21.

Fisher, Max. "The dividing of a continent: Africa's separatist problem." *Atlantic*, September 10, 2012.

Global Study on Homicide 2013. United Nations Office on Drugs and Crime (UNODC), March 2014.

"International Court of Justice gives judgment in Cameroon-Nigeria boundary dispute." International Court of Justice press release, October 10, 2002. www.un.org/press/en/2002/icj603.doc.htm.

"Land and maritime boundary between Cameroon and Nigeria." The Hague Justice Portal. www.haguejusticeportal.net/index.php?id=6220.

Onuoha, Mimi. "A 5-mile island built to save Lagos's economy has a worrying design flaw." *Quartz Africa*, March 18, 2007.

Pearce, Fred. "The African queen." *New Scientist*, September 11, 1999.

"Yoruba kingdoms—Benin and Ife." GlobalSecurity.org. Accessed December 12, 2017. www.globalsecurity.org/military/world/africa/yoruba.htm.

CHAPTER 7: EUROPE

"Attitudes towards immigration in Europe: Myths and realities." European Social Survey, European Parliament, June 19, 2017. www.europeansocialsurvey.org/docs/findings/IE_Handout_FINAL.pdf.

Judt, Tony. *A Grand Illusion? An Essay on Europe.* New York and London: New York University Press, 2011.

Katz, Bruce, Luise Noring, and Nantke Garrelts. "Cities and refugees: The German experience." Washington, DC: Brookings Institution, September 18, 2016.

Lambert, Charles. "French immigration problems." *Foreign Affairs,* January 1928.

Leuenberger, Christine. "Constructions of the Berlin Wall: How material culture is used in psychological theory." *Social Problems* 53, no. 1 (February 2006): 18–37.

Pew-Templeton Global Religious Futures Project. Pew Research Center report, 2010.

Ross, Corey. "East Germans and the Berlin Wall: Popular opinion and social change before and after the border closure of August 1961." *Journal of Contemporary History* 39, no. 1 (January 2004): 25–43.

Stein, Mary Beth. "The politics of humor: The Berlin Wall in jokes and graffiti." *Western Folklore* 48, no. 2 (April 1989): 85–108.

Steinmetz, Vanessa. "Das sollen Flüchtlinge künftig leisten." *Spiegel Online,* May 24, 2016.

CHAPTER 8: UK

Bruce, John Collingwood. *The Roman Wall.* London: J. R. Smith, 1851.

Divine, David. *Hadrian's Wall: The North-West Frontier of Rome.* New York: Barnes and Noble, 1995.

Nolan, Paul. "Two tribes: A divided Northern Ireland." *Irish Times,* April 1, 2017.

"Population of the UK by country of birth and nationality: 2015." Office for National Statistics, August 25, 2016.

Torney, Kathryn. "How integrated are the schools where you live?" *Detail,* November 23, 2012.

United Kingdom 2011 Census. Office for National Statistics. www.ons.gov.uk/census/2011census.

Index

Page numbers in *italics* refer to illustrations.

US-Mexican Border Wall, 3, 37–68, *40*
Uzbekistan, 2

Vaishyas, 148–49
Vanguard, 170
varnas (social classes), 150
Varosha, 248
VAT (value-added tax), 228
Venerable Bede, 224
Vietnam, 49, 64, 206, 240
Vietnam War, 49, 64
Violent Borders (Jones), 43
virtual private networks (VPNs), 30, 31
visas, 52
Visegrád Group, 199
Vision 2030 economic model, 116

Wade, George, 224–25
wahnsinnig ("mind-blowing"), 191
Wales, 222, 223, 229, 246
Wallace, Mike, 28
"Walled Off Hotel," 74–75
Wall of Shame, 157, 158, 176, 187
"wall peckers," 191
walls:
    agriculture and, 16, 26, 27, 135–37, 175
    assimilation, 62–63, 81, 208–9, 242
    authoritarianism encouraged by, 18, 107, 113–16, 245
    as barbed-wire fences, 2, 48, 49, 73, 111, 125–26, 128, 131, 185, 187, 248–49
    as border controls, 4, 101, *124,* 126, 132, 133, 137, 146–47, 152, 169–70, 185–88, 191, 198, 202–3, 233–34, 247, 248–50
    border deaths on account of, 126, 132, 152
    border guards for, 4, 101, *124,* 126, 132, 133, 137, 146, 185–86, 187, 188, 191, 248–49
    as buffer zones, 6, 20, 46, 111, 146, 178, 248
    cease-fires and, 76, 143, 145
    checkpoints for, 54, 73, 74, 101, 135, 194, 249
    citizenship and, 26, 27, 46, 48, 53, 87, 94, 132, 133, 138, 146, 204, 206, 210, 221, 237, 244, 251
    civilization defined by, 4, 15, 16, 22, 43, 221–25, 255

    colonialism and development of, 7, 114, 127, 157–58, *165,* 166, 179–80
    as concrete barriers, 1, 5, 42, 45, 56–57, 58, 73–74, 101–3, 110, 128, 146, 185, 187–88, 194, 231, 252
    cyber security and, 9, 31, 32–35
    deportations aided by, 44–45, 48, 51, 52, 80–81, 132, 134
    in developing countries, 62, 132, 253–54
    dismantling of, 1, 2, 15, *181,* 185–95, 196, 211, 237
    diversity hampered by, 3, 63, 206, 214, 240, 242–44
    economic impact of, 6, 7, 16, 21–25, 29–36, 48, 49, 51–58, 83, 86, 87, 92, 108, 112, 114, 116, 128, 132, 138, 168, 171, 172, 175, 187–93, 196, 198, 203, 209, 212, 214, 222, 231, 232, 237, 238, 250, 254
    as electric fences, 4, 73, 125, 173, 175, 187
    ethnic divisions and, 7, 13, 16, 20, 21, 44, 52, 58–68, 81, 88, 107, 108, 117, 118, 119, 127, 131, 138, 139, 159, 160, 164–72, 178, 179, 205, 209, 210, 226, 239, 240, 244, 252, 254
    freedom denied by, 9, 31, 36, 68, 114–16, 130, 205–6, 241–42, 255
    for gated communities, 175–78
    historical development of, 1–7
    for immigration control, 2, 4, 41, 43, 44, 46, 48–54, 58, 59, 63, 80, 112, 127, 128, 131, 132–34, 137, 139, 158, 173, 174, 200, 202–4, 208, 209, 211–15, 238–42, 252, 254
    for land disputes, 76–78, 83, 88, 93, 167
    laws and legal issues for, 9, 31, 32–35, 49, 52, 93, 169–70, 227, 252; *see also specific laws and treaties*
    maps of, *19, 24, 47, 59, 77, 89, 106, 107, 129, 136, 161, 165, 189, 197, 235*
    nationalism and, 1, 2, 5, 6, 7, 43, 44, 45, 58, 63–65, 68, 81, 88, 113–19, 130, 131, 135, 141, 142, 146, 147, 159–69, 172–80, 195, 198–200, 209, 210, 214, 225–33, 238, 240, 245, 246, 251–56
    national security and, 2, 45, 53, 57, 109, 126, 132, 134, 141–42, 149, 181

About the Author

Tim Marshall is a leading authority on foreign affairs with more than twenty-five years of reporting experience. He was diplomatic editor at Sky News and before that worked for the BBC. He has reported from forty countries and covered conflicts in Croatia, Bosnia, Macedonia, Kosovo, Afghanistan, Iraq, Lebanon, Syria, and Israel. He is the author of the *New York Times* bestseller *Prisoners of Geography: Ten Maps That Explain Everything About the World* and *A Flag Worth Dying For: The Power and Politics of National Symbols*, the first two books in his Politics of Place series. He is founder and editor of the current affairs site TheWhatandtheWhy.com.